A Course in Life

A Course in Life

The Twelve Universal Principles for Achieving a Life Beyond Your Dreams

Joan Gattuso

JEREMY P. TARCHER/PUTNAM
a member of Penguin Putnam Inc.
New York

Most Tarcher/Putnam books are available at special quantity discounts for bulk purchase for sales promotions, premiums, fund-raising, and educational needs. Special books or book excerpts also can be created to fit specific needs. For details, write Putnam Special Markets, 375 Hudson Street, New York, NY 10014.

Jeremy P. Tarcher/Putnam
A member of
Penguin Putnam Inc.
375 Hudson Street
New York, NY 10014
www.penguinputnam.com

First trade paperback edition 1999

Published simultaneously in Canada

Library of Congress Cataloging-in-Publication Data

Gattuso, Joan M.
A course in life : the twelve universal principles for achieving a life beyond your dreams / Joan Gattuso.
p. cm.
ISBN 0-87477-965-0 (alk. paper)
1. Spiritual life. 2. Conduct of life. 3. Success. I. Title.
BL624.G365 1998 97-29372 CIP
291.4′4—dc21

Book design by Ralph Fowler
Photograph of the author on page 227 by Strauss-Peyton

Printed in the United States of America

10 9 8 7 6 5 4 3 2 1

This book is printed on acid-free paper. ♾

With love and eternal gratitude
I dedicate this book to my parents,

JIM AND VIVIAN GATTUSO

You have always loved me deeply
and supported me fully.
You are extraordinary.

Contents

A Course in Life

Introduction

From my earliest memory, the things of the Spirit and the desire to lead a spiritual life have been of utmost importance to me. As a little girl I was very devout and loved going to daily Mass. That was a habit I continued through college and into my early twenties. I was always a seeker, pondering the mysteries of life from an early age. Within my religion, however, there were few options open for women, especially searching, questioning young women.

Around the age of twenty, I often visited the parish priest who served as clergyman for students at the college in southern Ohio I was attending. We would sit in his study after Mass, and I would ask him the questions rising from my soul. I was filled with questions about the "mysteries of the church." I believed the priest would have the answers. But instead of getting answers, I was reprimanded for having such inquisitive thoughts. "You *should not* be thinking about such things," he told me. "But I *am* thinking about such things," I objected. "Well, it's all a mystery and you must accept that on faith," he said. "Stop troubling yourself with such matters. Just stop thinking so much."

I did not realize it at the time, but that day was clearly the beginning of the end of my association with the traditional church. I continued to question and ponder, to search for answers. I had some glimpses of a fuller, richer spiritual reality than I had been taught about within the narrow margins of the religion of my ancestors. I knew there had to be more to God and church than what was being communicated by the religious hierarchy.

Several years would pass before I began to find any answers. Initially the very idea of ever leaving the Catholic Church was inconceivable to me. However by the time I was in my early twenties, my soul began to stir and I was gently led into something new and provocative, exciting and satisfying. I found myself encouraged to question and explore, study and tune in to my own being for answers. The difference was remarkable: instead of "Stop thinking so much," I heard "Your thoughts are the building blocks of your world." I was like a long-dry sponge that had been thirsting for spiritual nourishment about to be filled with water for the soul. Here I was, learning about the goodness of God dwelling within me, about being a co-creator capable of being conscious in the activity of co-creating. I was coming to understand that God was not a big guy in the sky with a measuring stick and a ledger, but a loving spirit inherent in all of life, and that no single religious school or institution had access to the one Spirit, that God could be recognized through his spiritual codes, through divine Universal Principles.

I passionately sought out these Universal Principles, the underpinnings of all great spiritual thought. It was remarkably energizing to learn that spiritual truths taught by Jesus had been taught by the Buddha before Him, and could be found not only in the stories of the Old and New Testaments but in countless other teachings and sacred scriptures as well. These great Spiritual Laws, although found within religious teachings, were not contained within the domain of religion. They expanded beyond the collective body of religious thought and moved into and through the very soul of each one of us. Most important, these Universal Principles could be reached from within our own hearts. I was on fire! My life would never be the same. Here were remarkable spiritual tools that could be an unshakable foundation for anyone willing to explore their depths and practice being a co-creator with God.

In the ensuing years I studied with many teachers, drinking from wells of knowledge of numerous spiritual traditions, including Judaism, mystical Christianity, Buddhism, Hinduism, Sufism, and Hawaiian Huna, as well as ancient mystery religions and Native American spirituality. I found during these years of learning and exploration that there were many paths to the divine, and although they may have looked different, though they may have different emphases, they contained a common thread of Universal Spiritual Wisdom. Even among those that focused on ritual and form and at times seemed to lose the underlying spiritual truth, that Wisdom could still be found.

In all the ten directions of the universe,
There is only one truth.
When we see clearly, the great teachings are all the same.

RYOKAN

Spiritual Principles are not exclusive to any one religious institution, time, or hierarchy. They are written within the soul of each one of us, and we are capable of becoming aware of them, living from them, and empowering our lives with them.

A Course in Life encourages you to view all of life in an inclusive way. You will begin to discern that the instructions of the world's greatest spiritual teachers and greatest minds bear a single golden thread that has been exquisitely woven throughout the ages for us all. They guide us into a higher, deeper, fuller understanding of our spiritual nature and our relationship with God and with all of life.

In all spiritual teachings there is the message that we and the divine are one. *A Course in Life* seeks to clarify how we can awaken to these Spiritual Laws, and use them every moment of our lives.

Buddhists speak of engaging their Buddhism. In this book, let us together journey into an engaged spirituality, no longer nodding in passive agreement or mumbling meaningless memorized prayers out of obligation, but instead fully investing our innate spirituality. Engaging our spirituality is the recurring theme of this book. *A Course in Life* offers a way to live as a Spiritual Being governed by Spiritual Laws living in a Spiritual Universe.

Through the years many seekers have asked me what books define these Spiritual Laws or Universal Principles. Although there are many inspiring works with teachings that reflect Universal Laws, I have always been at a loss to name a book that describes and explains what these Laws are, why they are Laws, what makes them Universal and Spiritual, and what impact they could have on our lives.

Feeling the lack of such a book, I knew I needed to write it: a key to living a spiritually actualized life. Thus *A Course in Life.*

A mammoth inscription on a wall of the Jefferson Memorial in Washington, D.C., quotes from Jefferson's *The Life and*

Morals of Jesus of Nazareth. It reads: "New Truths discovered. We do not create that which is spiritually true, but we merely discover for ourselves that which has always been the truth."

You are a Spiritual Being, living in a Spiritual Universe, governed by Spiritual Law, and you can discover and use these Laws to create an extraordinary life. You are a creation of God and were created good. You were created in love to express love. The key to unlock the door of your life is to uncover, recognize, and use the Spiritual Laws so your life works, and works with beauty and grace all of the time. You will then live in the goodness of life.

Spiritual Laws are how God defines the universe as what it is. Spiritual Laws are what has always been true and will forever remain true. They are the means by which God's Laws are upheld within the universe.

Spiritual Laws are what those recovering from various addictions study and endeavor to live by in twelve-step programs. Spiritual Laws lie deep within the soul and address our true nature and ultimate reality.

Spiritual Laws are the omnipresent, universal activity of the Creator through us, the created. By working with these Universal Laws, we bring the Divine into our moment-to-moment existence.

No one has a corner on these Universal Truths. Rather, all great spiritually realized men and women have lived in accord with them. Living a life in harmony with these Truths builds an unshakable foundation of trust in our innate goodness, builds faith in God's presence everywhere, and in our divine heritage and inheritance. Spiritual Laws are the core values from which we live our lives.

Contained in the teachings of all great men and women of the spirit are recurring patterns for living. Some are obvious; others, no less important, are more subtle in revealing themselves.

Jesus, Moses, the Buddha, Krishna, Mohammed, great saints of India, Christian and Sufi mystics, and great philosophers, prophets, and shamans lived and taught out of underlying Truths of Being. As we individually awaken from our long slumber in mortal consciousness, we come to recognize that these core Truths are not just for the great men and women of antiquity. The outer expression of these Truths varies according to time, tradition, audience, and, yes, even consciousness. But the Universal Truths themselves remain the same: They can connect all of us with the same awakened knowledge of the universality of life and our oneness with the Divine.

This book will clearly define these Universal Spiritual Laws, explain them in depth, and illustrate how and why they are fundamental Laws of Being. I will also explain how you can fully engage these same great Truths in your own life so they become your foundation of being. Throughout *A Course in Life* we shall dive into the deep waters of Spiritual Truth and explore through lesson, illustration, and exercises twelve fundamental Universal Laws of Being. Here are the twelve Spiritual Laws:

1. Faith. This is the great Spiritual Truth that each of us is constantly creating our own view of reality. We all have faith, although sometimes it may be misdirected. The good news is, if life isn't working well, we can create it another way.
2. Divine purpose. A Divine plan is encoded within each of us. When we are attuned to this plan, life flows and unfolds magnificently. We have all been created for a mighty purpose.

3. Consciousness. Here you will learn this unfailing law, what it constitutes, and how to clear yours.
4. Vision. The blind can see. Seeing isn't solely through the physical eyes. You can awaken to inner sight and have reality revealed to you. Learn to set things right in your world through spiritual vision.
5. Joy. Learn to lighten up. You are blessed beyond measure. You were created to know joy and live a happy life. You will learn how to increase your own joy and make it, rather than pain, a constant in your life.
6. Power. By using your spiritual power, you get out of "poor me." There is an awesome, untapped power within you. You were born with it. Learn how to release it to create the kind of life you have always dreamed of.
7. Love. Love isn't something you receive, it is something you *are.* Learn to harmonize your life with the pure essence of love. As you remove the blocks to your love, life becomes more and more magnificent.
8. Wisdom. You can simplify your life by merely paying attention to the obvious. Your Higher Self is always one with God, constantly guiding you. You'll learn how to hear this direction and put it to use in your life.
9. Non-attachment. This is not disinterest. Since you are not journeying through the cosmos alone, tremendous assistance is ever available. Your individual role is to learn to ask and accept the help that is always at hand.
10. Abundance. You may not be aware of it, but there is unlimited abundance in the universe. You can learn ways to develop and deepen your own consciousness of prosperity. You will discover how to become master of both giving and receiving.

11. Forgiveness. When you forgive, you do forget. Eliminating what doesn't work in your life by forgiving it clears the way for attracting your good. When you learn what letting go really means, you will experience all the good that rushes in to fill the vacuum.
12. Divine life. When you uncoil your sleeping life force, you awaken a giant within. You may then fill yourself with universal vitality and begin to live a life that reflects the divinity you uncover.

The study and practice of Spiritual Laws must appeal to your intellect and your heart alike. For me a great excitement came when I began to study these Universal Laws, because I was encouraged to think, to question, to explore intellectually as well as to feel. I was experiencing them within my heart and soul, not just with my head.

It was my thinking and questioning mind that could not accept rote answers as the truth that led me to explore spiritual life outside the walls of any formal religion. As Emerson wrote, "When we have broken with our God of tradition and ceased to worship the God of our intellect, God fires us with His presence."

These Universal Laws fire us with the presence of God. They are often compared to the principles of mathematics, physics, or music, for they are just as knowable, consistent, and reliable. We can trust these principles to be true even when we do not have a fully developed awareness of them.

We would not, for instance, criticize a six-year-old's addition or subtraction as an inadequate expression of the laws of mathematics because the child does not know or demonstrate a knowledge of calculus or trigonometry. And if a child—or even an adult—comes up with an incorrect answer to a math problem, that answer does not alter the principles of mathematics.

The underlying principles of mathematics are not altered by the demonstrator. They do not favor one student over another or one people over another. They simply are. They are impersonal, consistent, universal. They are the same in Honolulu or Paris or Sydney or Tel Aviv. If there is an error in their elaboration, it is the result of some misapplication of a principle by a student, not, as some students might protest, some error in the principle.

The Universal Laws are just as reliable as those that underlie our daily living. We are aware of the laws common to the physical side of life: Gravity attracts all objects, whether brick, baseball, toaster, or feather. Water will seek its own level, whether it's in a teakettle or the Pacific Ocean. The angles of a triangle always add up to 180 degrees—no exceptions. Light travels at 186,000 miles per second. This pertains to any source—the sun, a flashlight, a lamp. These physical laws always work, and our understanding of them has nothing to do with their working or not. Our understanding dictates only whether or not we will use these physical laws consciously in our physical lives.

The same is true for the Spiritual Laws governing our spiritual lives. If we accept that we are spiritual beings having a human experience, we can discover and attune ourselves to these demonstrable Spiritual Principles, which always work.

Through study and practice, we can demonstrate to the full measure the physical principles. So too can we come to live conscious lives with Spiritual Principles as the foundation of our being, and demonstrate them fully as well.

The study of these Laws has long been the domain of the mystic and the metaphysician, but as we as a species are speeding into a new millennium, countless individuals are awakening and want to know more about the fundamental cause of being. In the massive confusion produced in our dark and separated state, we have forgotten we were created by God. The confusion in our lost minds tells us we created ourselves; we forever remove God from the equation, and believe we were capable of usurping the power of God. But as *A Course in Miracles,* a profound modern spiritual text on awakening to our ultimate reality, states, "You have not usurped the power of God, but you have lost it. Fortunately to lose something does not mean that it is gone."

Our function is to discover and accept that which is already ours from God's creation. We must also release the pain and suffering we made for ourselves in an attempt to replace God's Laws with our own.

Spiritual Principles uphold God's Laws within the Universe. They are the foundation upon which our heritage as divine sons and daughters is built. As we study them, we can, as Jefferson said, discover "that which has always been the truth."

With tenacity and perseverance, I practiced these Spiritual Laws and moved out of dysfunctional, insane relationships into sane, holy ones. I moved from a diagnosis in my early twenties of chronic low energy to a life of remarkable vitality; from living a life filled with upsets, struggle, and heartache to one that is joyous, experiencing heaven here and now.

It was Lao-tzu, the ancient Chinese sage, who said, "My words are very easy to understand." The Spiritual Laws presented here must be integrated to have any true meaning or impact. They are clear, simple, provable. They are very easy to understand when we have eyes to see and ears to hear. Then we can accept that we can demystify the mystical and live here and now the glorious, fully engaged life we were created to live. We will learn to live out of love and joy and to co-create blessed states of being rather than remain in unhappiness and suffering.

Is it really possible to live such a wondrous life? Absolutely! What one can achieve, all can achieve, if the desire is there and the way is shown. My prayer is that you desire a fuller, richer life for yourself. By incorporating the principles of *A Course in Life* into your being, you can embrace your own innate spirituality. Use these teachings as a road map back home to God. May every blessing shower round about you.

With love,
Joan Gattuso

The Discovery Channel

The Spiritual Law of Faith

I

In the movie *It Could Happen to You,* the character played by Nicolas Cage, finding himself short of cash and in want of a tip, promises a coffee shop waitress, played by Bridget Fonda, half of his lottery winnings if he should have the winning ticket. Of course that is exactly what happens. Cage's character wins the New York State Lottery, and being an honest, middle-class chap, he remembers his promise and sets about keeping it. His wife, played by Rosie Perez, is a woman without much depth and is furious with her husband.

The Cage and Fonda characters both literally "miss the boat" for a New York State Lottery winners' bash. They decide to share dinner as they wait for the party boat to return to the dock. Over dinner Cage's character describes his wife and their relationship. He expresses it perfectly when he says, "I'm CNN. She's the Home Shopping Network."

If you had only a quick moment to name your channel, what

would it be? Would you choose a major network, Fox, the Playboy Channel, American Movie Classics, ESPN, Disney, Lifetime, or the Discovery Channel? Our consciousness has access to a vast number of inner channels. We have total control over which channel or channels we align our inner selves with. There are channels that we can attune ourselves to that will always create heartache and pain. There are meaningless channels, drama-queen channels, thrill-seeker channels, and crisis channels. But there are also success channels, ease channels, fulfillment channels, and peaceful, happy channels. Until we begin to mature spiritually, we deny our own involvement in tuning in, be it to the suffering channel or the happy channel.

On the Suffering Channel, we believe in the reality of suffering and we recite a litany of wrongs, slights, and injustices that have been inflicted on us. While stuck on this channel we are in chains, not because life has imprisoned us, but because we believe that unhappiness is our lot. As long as we are tuned to the Suffering Channel, we are misdirecting a great spiritual power, our ability to direct the law of faith according to the desires of our hearts. It sounds insane to think that our desires of the heart could ever be misery and suffering. It not only sounds insane, but is insane. It is out of a very inverted perception and mindless choices that innumerable lost souls are stuck on the Suffering Channel; they have directed their energy toward that negative channel. *A Course in Miracles* tells us, "Faith can keep the Son of God [that's you] in chains as long as he believes he is in chains." We have misused our ability to create, and in our upside-down thinking not only are we misusing our power and placing it in the negative, but also we are disassociating ourselves from the entire process. This is amazing—and insane. Jesus said, "According to your faith is it done unto you."

We believe awful things keep happening to us, denying that they are happening *through* us. We have to acknowledge that they are happening not *to* us, but *through* us as a result of our thoughts, beliefs, and faith.

Elaine is a woman who lives in misery, stuck on the Suffering Channel. She grew up a sheltered child and received the lesson from her mother that a woman's role was to fill everyone else's needs and rescue them from themselves. After finishing college Elaine married a mainline Protestant minister, despite the fact her inner voice told her he was not her perfect partner. As she reflects over the past twenty-five years, she speaks of knowing she should have listened to her inner voice the night before the wedding and called it off then and there. Sadly, she had neither the courage to trust her inner voice nor the faith to follow her inner guidance. The next morning, sobbing, she walked down the aisle. Over the next decade the marriage produced four children, and the family went through the motions of a normal life.

Then five years ago the illusion was shattered, when Elaine's husband broke down and admitted to her that he was homosexual and was in love with an Eastern Orthodox priest. Her husband was also drinking heavily, and his alcoholism, with all the related co-dependency problems, became their reality. Elaine's husband eventually joined Alcoholics Anonymous, and Elaine realized she needed to face her problem of co-dependency. In the midst of this upheaval, Elaine's widowed mother, who was her one supporter and anchor, died. Elaine felt she had nowhere to go and no resources, yet she had to protect her children and maintain the façade of the normal family and her role as the pastor's wife. There she was, planning church socials and the children's church program, holding up the front of the happy,

> The state of faith allows no mention of impossibility.
>
> ·TERTULLIAN·

well-adjusted religious family, while her husband was gone for several days with his lover. Her life was a nightmare.

Elaine tried several business and professional ventures. While pursuing one of these she met a man who paid attention to her, cared for her and encouraged her, and she came close to having an affair. As the complexity of the ego would have it, this man was married to a minister who was a lesbian. Needless to say, they had no sex life, and he very much desired Elaine, as she desired him. When she saw how complex things were, Elaine retreated. She is still living with her now sober homosexual husband. She thinks of him as a friend and parent to their children, but not as a husband. She is unhappy, unfulfilled, and suffering. Elaine could choose another channel, but she doesn't realize it. She sees herself as stuck with four children, no money, and no surviving family. I have spoken to her again and again about how God's plan is not for any of us to live a lie or to live in misery. She does have a strong faith in God and is trying to learn how to apply it in a practical, life-supporting way.

God does not want Elaine to suffer and live in a sexless marriage, covering up for her husband daily. There are no jewels given out on this plane of existence for living the most miserable life, nor will there be any on the next. Many people justify their misery by believing that they are doing the godly thing by not divorcing, choosing instead to remain in a loveless state. At any moment of her life Elaine could have changed to the Discovery Channel, and she still can. If and when she does, she will realize and live a far richer, more rewarding, love-filled life.

When I first read Richard Bach's classic *Illusions*, I committed to memory my favorite verses:

The world is your exercise book
The pages on which you do your sums
It is not reality although you can express reality here
if you wish
Or you can write nonsense or tear up the pages.

In this book we shall explore how to tune in to the true reality, which from now on I will refer to as "Reality," with a capital R. Imagine an enormous dial set in the center of a huge wheel, with zones marked Belief, Trust, Victimhood, Faith, Goodness, Evil, Heartache, Joy, and Love. Each one of us gets a screen, and we choose which zone will be programmed onto our individual screen—except it's not really a screen, it's our life. We are continuously creating our own reality. Our greatest discovery is that we are making it all up. Once we awaken to this truth, we can begin to live in a pleasing and fulfilling way.

Let's click on Kaye's life and watch a few scenes of her view of reality. Kaye, the mother of two teenagers, is thirty-nine but acts twenty years older. Her friends, after years of trying to be supportive, are pulling away, saying they are tired of attempting to support a woman who does not want support, but wants only to complain.

Her entire life Kaye has played the role of a long-suffering martyr. As a child, the middle of five, she loathed her controlling mother, who had no friends and complained constantly about her husband. Kaye swore she would never be like her mother, but it is no surprise that she is becoming just like her. Kaye has few friends, complains constantly, alienates her children, and draws herself toward increasingly more negative situations. She

> Believe that you have it, and you have it.
>
> ·DESIDERIUS ERASMUS·

believes she is powerless over her life, and because she believes it, it has become her Reality.

In order for Kaye to get off the Suffering Channel, first she needs to recognize that her negativity and her persistent focus on being a victim are powerful and self-destructive, and they are keeping her in misery. Second, she needs to choose another course for her life. Choosing to give up being the martyr isn't always easy when it's become a lifelong habit, but it is the only way to have peace instead of conflict, and forgiveness instead of hatred. Kaye has to choose to focus on the ray of light and hope rather than on retelling her tale of woe. If Kaye made such choices, she would find her intolerable situation begin to change.

The real question is whether Kaye wants to be released from the bondage of her suffering more than she wants to play the role of the long-suffering, dutiful, unappreciated daughter who is the victim of her mother's outrageous demands and unkind spirit. Kaye has other possibilities before her, but while she is stuck in being the victim, tuned to the Suffering Channel, she cannot use these options.

What We Focus on Expands

Here is one of the simplest and greatest Spiritual Principles: The very activity of our thoughts focused on a particular memory, idea, or outcome extends that thought from itself outward, and as it extends outward, it expands. In *A Course in Miracles,* this teaching is explained: "Every thought extends because that is its purpose." Whether we recognize it or not, we have the power to choose what we think about, what we focus on in our thoughts.

Our focus is an activity of faith. We can be like Elaine or Kaye, misusing our power of faith to focus on the negative. Yet we seldom recognize that it is of our own making, that we are the ones creating our negative reality. The faith we give to the negative, hurtful, and cruel does not lack power. We join God as the co-creator of our Reality, consciously or unconsciously. The choice is up to each one of us. None of us lacks faith. What we lack is an understanding of what to do with our faith. We need to learn how to use it in ways that increase our ability to welcome ease and joy into our lives. A simple analogy may help you understand how faith works.

"Faith Is Like Tofu"

Today tofu is very popular and is used in a variety of ways, but when I first attempted to cook with it, it wasn't in such wide usage. I remember buying a block of the beige stuff without any idea what to do with it. I asked a friend, who told me, "You can do anything you want with it." Well, that sounded easy enough. Since I wanted it hot, I sliced it and put it in a 350-degree oven for several minutes, and then sat down to eat it. It was ghastly! I was unable to swallow it.

The next day I asked a fellow vegetarian whether he ever ate tofu and, if so, how he prepared it, because mine was surely awful. When I told him what I had done he burst out laughing, then patiently explained that tofu absorbs the flavor of whatever is put with it, but it has to be put with *something.*

Put it with nothing and it's tasteless. Put it in Indonesian peanut sauce and it takes on that flavor. Put it with Caribbean spices and it takes on those flavors. Tofu absorbs whatever it is partnered with. And that's how faith is like tofu: it absorbs whatever we partner it with. So we should partner it with life-affirming thoughts that have an expanding effect. We will then have what we desire expanding in our lives.

A Course in Miracles tells us that whenever we suffer, experience loss or fear, or are dissatisfied with the outcome of a given event, it is because that outcome is what we thought we deserved.

If things never "work out" for us, it's because we are misusing our faith and internally and externally declaring that life is miserable and never works out for us. Whatever is present in your life now is there because at some point in the past you opened your mind and said, "Come in." Many people may be skeptical: "Why would I ever welcome this godawful situation?" they wonder. We must reverse our existing beliefs, discard our old, limited helpless-victim states of mind and models of living. We realize we have a choice, and can and must choose another course for ourselves if we are ever going to be happy.

There is another way to view this principle. Rather than "godawful," view it as remarkably positive and freeing. If we have been and continue to be the creators of our present Reality, then the *really* great news is that we can learn to stop creating such havoc. When we do, we can use our faith to focus on what we desire. This time we will attract a Reality that is soul-nurturing and life-affirming.

For each of us, the world we see is the world we want to see. Remember Richard Bach's line, "It is not reality." God did not create the world you see. You have the power to create true *Reality* here if you wish. In order to do so, you will have to look, and look deeply, into where you have been directing your faith. As we use our self-directed faith, joined with the divine, we realize how splendid our lives can become.

> Faith in an all-seeing and personal God elevates the soul, purifies the emotions, sustains human dignity, and lends poetry, nobility, and holiness to the commonest state, condition, and manner of life.
>
> ·JUAN VALERA·

The Universal Law simply stated is this: We all have faith. Where we individually place it determines what we see and the results we experience. I have studied this teaching a number of times, from several spiritual perspectives. The workbook of *A Course in Miracles* reads, "Decide but to accept your rightful place as co-creator of the universe, and all you think you made will disappear." What rises to our awareness will be all that is eternally true. This spiritualized eternal awareness will take the place of self-deception. It is here that eternal truth arises to replace self-deception. This is where we need to place our faith and begin consciously to withdraw it from the frightening pictures we have made. This is exactly what Elaine and Kaye must do to free themselves from their unhappiness. As our understanding of faith and how it operates grows, we are learning to empower ourselves. The loving yet powerful Vietnamese monk and author Thich Nhat Hanh says, "Our faith must be alive, growing like a tree." Your power of faith has been established by God. What you choose to do with it is up to you. Nurture it, use it wisely, and it will grow like a tree of great strength and comfort within you.

What we realize when we turn to the Discovery Channel is that *we* are powerful beyond measure.

> Faith is the substance of things hoped for,
> the evidence of things not seen.
>
> ·BOOK OF HEBREWS·

Belief

Faith is to believe what we do not see, and the reward of such faith is to see what we believe.

ST. AUGUSTINE

Belief is not the same as faith, but is a step in a new direction. It is a primary tool and a necessary one for tilling our minds. It is the first tool we must familiarize ourselves with on our journey toward an understanding of faith. The Buddhists call this first level "attraction." Our belief in the *possibility* is the first assignment we must make with the spirit within. Here we begin to be attracted to our good.

"You'll see it when you believe it," best-selling author Wayne Dyer has written. The long-held thought of limited thinkers has been the opposite: "I'll believe it when I see it." This is a perfect example of how much of the world thinks, a false, upside-down view of reality that masses have gathered around. But it's not the truth. It is an example of how, in our ignorant states of mind, we can invert the truth and then cling to false concepts.

The spiritual truth is that whatever we believe is what we see. The fact that we believe something gives it credence in our minds, importance in our lives. Dyer's observation is accurate. We do see "it," whatever "it" is for us, because we believe "it." Nothing ever shows up in our lives before we believe in its reality. Our belief in the good and true grows through spiritual study or inspirational teachings, through an awakening insight or a quickening in the heart, from a message in a book, by prayer, from a teacher. Belief is thus quickened and will bring results. The challenge with these results is that they are sporadic. With belief alone, we will make some progress, but its manifestations are neither consistent nor one hundred percent reliable. Belief gets us moving in the right direction, toward the Discovery Channel, but there is a lot of interference and static. Though the picture isn't clear, we can see some images and we begin to come to an understanding, however limited, that we are having an impact on our reality, that we are actually in charge.

As our belief in the possible grows, our demonstrations of good increase as well. As we continue to cultivate belief within our minds, our thoughts consistently turn toward the positive of what could be, and our hearts are more willing and open to the divine. It is now that our belief begins to mature into the next stage, trust.

Trust

These first two stages, belief and trust, can be likened to a child's experience in learning to ride a bicycle. Try to remember that time for you: Before you could ride a two-wheeler, you saw other children doing so. If it was possible for them, on some level you must have accepted the idea that it was possible for you. Enter belief. When you began to ride, you either had training wheels or someone assisting you in balancing yourself. Enter trust. You had to trust that person or those training wheels, and with practice you came to trust your own ability to balance and the entire experience of riding. You probably did not understand the dynamics of balance, but you did understand that certain feeling of being in balance. Now, even if you haven't climbed on a bike in years, if the opportunity presented itself, without a thought you would *trust* the process, climb on, and ride away.

Trust emerges after we have had a sufficient number of demonstrations using our expanding belief in the goodness of life. The Buddhists refer to this level as "confidence." We relax a bit; we exhale and rely on this principle more and more. We trust it to work through us and for us. Once we move into trust, we find much less static on our channel. We feel we can trust the Universal Principle; we feel that it is real, that it is there for us and will support us, like a friend who keeps his word and commitments. Such a friend never lets you down. When he says he'll be happy to help you and pick up your children after school, you feel confident in turning that responsibility over to him.

Even if we feel trust, we can occasionally experience doubt, uncertainty, and fear. Our trust can be rock-solid one moment, shaky the next. As we exercise this evolving consciousness, it is helpful to use meditation, study, spiritual disciplines, and affirmative prayer, and to practice letting go the need to control. All of this helps us move into our spiritual depths. Here and only here we can unite with our own realization of the Spiritual Law of faith, and develop an intimate relationship with faith.

Faith

My great realization of faith came six years ago, after I had been a minister for a dozen years and a practitioner of the Universal Principle for many more years than that. While coming out of anesthesia after surgery, I realized I was praying and affirming the wholeness of my mind and body—a total healing of my body.

During the surgery I had several lucid moments and had been listening to a tape of affirmations my husband, David, had made for me, his voice and mine. In those lucid moments, when I heard my voice I held the conscious thought, "Oh, that's my voice now." With the surgery in progress and my voice sounding through the headset, I affirmed and sent light and wisdom to the surgeon and all in attendance. Several days later, when I realized what had occurred, I knew my faith was much deeper than I had thought.

Faith in God. Faith in the Good. Faith in all things working together for good.

I had taken personal ownership of this divine principle. It was no longer just a beautiful theory; it was now my life, my Reality.

Faith is the formative energy of the divine in motion.

We must all take personal ownership of faith, not because someone taught it, because it is church dogma or someone else's idea, but because it is real to us. The Buddhists speak of this third level of faith as "irreversible." Faith has proven itself in our own experiences; it is our reliable, unfailing friend.

Progressive Affirmation

Here is a wonderful and faith-quickening way to awaken even more and move along in consciousness with your discovery of the power of faith.

> It is faith to believe that which you do not yet see; and the reward of faith is to see that which you believe.
>
> ·ST. AUGUSTINE·

> Those who have faith are prosperous; who are humble in their prayers, who turn away from idle talk, and who are active in almsgiving.
>
> ·KORAN·

Let's take Elaine, from earlier in the chapter, as an example. She might begin with an affirmation focused on belief, then proceed to trust, then advance to faith in her desired goal, and finally move into the full realization of this goal. Her progressive affirmation might look like this:

BELIEF

I, Elaine, am coming to believe that God desires only good and happiness for me.

Here she would write all the negative beliefs that this positive affirmation would push to the surface. Once Elaine's writing indicated that she agreed with the affirmation, she would move to the next stage.

TRUST

I, Elaine, now trust that God and I desire only good and happiness for me.

Again she would write any negative thoughts that surface, until she inwardly and outwardly agreed with the affirmation. Then she would move to the next stage.

FAITH

I, Elaine, now have faith that I deserve only good and happiness in my life.

She would clean out any remaining doubts and thoughts of being undeserving, of suffering, of being a victim. To strengthen herself and her faith further, she would move to the next stage.

ONENESS

I, Elaine, am faith.
I, Elaine, am deserving of only good.
I, Elaine, am now living a happy and fulfilled life.

In this final step, Elaine realizes her inner oneness with God and all of God's good.

The four stages of Progressive Affirmation are:

1. I believe.
2. I trust.
3. I have faith.
4. I am.

Work with the four stages in a particular area of your life. Don't begin with stage four if you've been experiencing any form of lack and limitation in your life.

The path to true faith is progressive. We cannot affirm "I have it all" when we believe God wants us to suffer or live in misery. We must accept that life has to offer us good and countless blessings. We must start with:

I believe I deserve to have increased good in my life,
to __________.

I trust God desires for me to have increased good in my life,
to __________.

I have faith that I am deserving, to __________.

I am deserving of only good in my life.

> The Faith of every man accords
> with his essential nature; man here is made up
> of faith; as a man's faith is, so is he.
>
> ·BHAGAVAD GITA·

It takes development and practice to move into the principle of faith, and once there we must be diligent to keep our faith alive, "growing like a tree," as Thich Nhat Hanh has said. Our faith must grow to meet the good that exists.

Quite often our challenge in growing is not in the setting of our good, but rather in the releasing of any known or unknown fears that block the desired good. A helpful practice in lifting ourselves out of our fears and into the desired good is to observe mindfully when any known fear is present. Fear can manifest itself in any number of emotional or physical ways—depression, dread, or foreboding; anxiety or excessive worry; a sense of tightness in the solar plexus, or heart palpitations, or perspiration. Fear is never a comfortable or pleasant feeling. Unknown or unrecognized buried fears may communicate their presence through such self-sabotage as injury to the body, quickness to anger, frequent excuses, and feelings of guilt and regret.

Releasing the Energy of Fear

Fear is the misuse of our faith by tuning it to the most negative of channels. To move fear out of our consciousness, we must consistently—faithfully—acknowledge its presence and then be willing to turn it over to the Higher Power, to God. Ask that all known and unknown fears that are clouding your vision and the realization of your goal be dissolved now and forever.

You might try a technique I particularly like: Take a half-hour in which you are alone. Find a comfortable place and position in which to sit. Rest your hands, cupped but open, on your lap and clear your mind by taking a deep and full breath. Expand your chest fully on the inhale, and exhale slowly and without force. Imagine your lungs as bellows filling with air, then releasing easily. This will aid you in going into a light meditative state. Slowly, one by one, with each inhalation bring to mind your known fears, and with a deep exhalation gently place each one in your palms. Do not hurry; do this exercise very mindfully. Imagine the fears joining together to form a solid mass in your cupped hands. Breathe into those known fears, and imagine the in-breath collecting them one by one; as you exhale, they gather in your palms. As you continue the exercise you may even feel a weight (I feel something like a ball) in your hands. Do the exercise long enough to sense the weight and the movement of energy; this may take fifteen minutes, perhaps longer.

Once you feel you have dealt with the known fears, you may begin to deal with the more subtle and unconscious ones. You may do much the same thing as above, now lifting one by one with each inhalation the unknown fears from the deeper realms of your consciousness and placing them in your palms with each exhalation. If you are doing this exercise effectively, you will continue to sense a weight gathering in your hands.

Now invite to come before you a symbol of the divine—an angel, or the Holy Spirit, for example. If a divine presence does not work for you, then visualize a clear, brilliant light. You can also call on the presence of Love itself. If you still cannot sense a presence within you, don't let it stop you. Your asking is enough. Now slowly lift your cupped hands with the collected mass of fears and give it away to this symbol of the divine, or this light.

You should feel a heaviness in your hands and a release of that heaviness as you willingly let it go. I have found this exercise is quite powerful, and very effective in sweeping out known and unknown fears, and many people I know have reported sensing not only a tremendous release, a lifting of long-held burdens, but also a quiet, holy presence enfolding them. As we process and remove the fears that have been blocking our desired good, our faith has room to grow; it can fill the places where the old fears dwelled.

There is a magnificent, glorious life waiting to emerge through you, and it is here for the asking. Your part is easy: all you need do is turn to the Discovery Channel and find out for yourself what it is like to live a life where your dreams do come true.

> Faith is the antiseptic of the soul.
>
> ·WALT WHITMAN·

Uncovering Your Purpose

The Spiritual Law of Divine Purpose

2

From *A Course in Miracles* and from the Dalai Lama I've learned that "our purpose is to be happy." If you're happy operating a jackhammer, great. If you're happy soaring through the clouds as a pilot, marvelous. If you're happy staying at home meditating six hours a day, wonderful. These are all fulfilling endeavors if they bring you joy. But when we are unhappy, we cannot align with our divine purpose, our true reason for being here. We are so busy living like frightened animals in a survival consciousness that our unhappiness clouds our vision. Instead of living in the present, we linger in the past or attempt to project ourselves into the future. We cannot know our purpose in either. Only when we come fully into the present moment can our divine purpose be revealed to us.

It was recently the fiftieth birthday of a woman I've known since we were teenagers. Lynn and I are no longer close, and had not seen each other for a number of years. I always remember

> Our birth is but a sleep and a forgetting;
> The Soul that rises with us, our life's star,
> Hath had elsewhere its setting,
> And cometh from afar;
> Not in entire forgetfulness,
> And not in utter nakedness,
> But trailing clouds of glory do we come
> From God, who is our home.
>
> ·WILLIAM WORDSWORTH·

her birthday, and thinking surely this one would be memorable for her, I knew I had to call. When I heard Lynn's voice on the phone, I exclaimed, "Happy birthday!"

She did not respond to my well-wishes, but instantly launched into her problems. "I have cysts in my breast, and I might have cancer." Before I could express my support she went on: "My oldest son was suspended from school. He was in a bicycle accident, and ever since he's had severe headaches. He lies constantly, he's a surly child. My husband lost his job in a buyout five months ago. He's trying to start a consulting business, but he's not having any luck. He's depressed and drinking too much. Our house is a mess. We were going to sell to cut expenses, but the capital gains tax would be a hundred thousand dollars. . . . I've gained thirty-five pounds."

On and on and on she went—telling me every ghastly detail of their miserable lives over the past several years. I finally wedged in a word and spoke of my concern for her plight. I reminded her how I had begun to use spiritual tools to create a wonderful life, to live out of a commitment to process negative beliefs and emotional baggage. "I don't know what you're talking about," she replied. I explained that this was a difficult part of life to delve into, and that it took a lot of work and commitment to process. But the results could be a life transformed. Again she said, "I don't know what you're talking about."

"I'm sure you don't," I answered. After she shared more tales of drama I told her, "I called to wish you happy birthday. I'm sorry that you're so unhappy and that your life is unmanageable. I have to go now, I have a flight to catch"—I actually did. I told her to call me if she wanted to look at her life in a different way. It was very difficult for me to end the conversation and release Lynn, rather than attempt to rescue her from her pain.

Lynn was orphaned at age six and was raised by doting relatives. She grew up with privilege, education, and money. She never thought it necessary to deal with her early trauma and losses and the emotional baggage. Today she is miserable, when she need not be. Lynn is so stuck in her story she can't grasp that she's creating it all and that she can learn to stop doing so. Lynn is living life totally disconnected from her core, constantly upset with her husband and son, hating her career, hating her life.

When we are heavily burdened by emotional baggage we create an unsatisfying life. We are always saying, "I don't want to do this. My kids are unmanageable. I'm a victim. I hate my job. I hate my life." All of these circumstances and more are crying out to Lynn, "Wake up!" But life does not have to be that way. When we are stuck in limited, little thinking, we cling to a job we cannot stand. We stay in that unrewarding job because we think that it is our security, the only one we could have. We are certain there is nothing else we could do that would reward us as much. In fact

> O, the fabulous wings unused
> Folded in the heart!
>
> ·CHRISTOPHER FRY·

there are thousands of things we could do that would provide us with more money—if that's what we're after—but then we wouldn't have our job to complain about. You can have joy and a sense of fulfillment while working to make a contribution to yourself and others. Lynn and her husband are mired in little thinking; they believe there are no other career opportunities for them. Their focus on misery keeps creating more and more misery. They do not comprehend their hidden splendor—that fulfillment and joy, not drama and crisis, is their due.

The outer expression of their inner splendor is unique to each of them, as it is to all; it will not match that of their friends, neighbors, or siblings; indeed, it will not match that between them. Yet buried within both Lynn and her husband is the ever-present possibility of living a beautiful life. They have the power to align their daily living with the unique, divine purpose for each of them.

One point on the eightfold path of Buddhism is Right Livelihood. This is a primary component of living one's divine purpose. Right Livelihood speaks of making one's life work helpful to other people. It is never harmful to anyone, and thus promotes one's own spiritual advancement.

When we discard our misery and victimhood, we begin to live, not merely survive. We connect with our own center and move into a unified field of being. Here we realize our connection with the pulse of life, a universal force that supports us in advancing toward our dreams. Here we are also connected with others, because we can celebrate with them the fulfillment of our individual divine purposes, knowing they could never interfere with one another. We can understand that we can also come to live our divine purpose. Thus are we inspired by others, and thus can we inspire others.

We must lift our sights above limitations and crisis, and focus on what might be. When we carry old baggage around, we are out of touch with what is possible. We are sleepwalking through our lives. Life is a struggle, every day a fight against the world—be it traffic or work or the children or inner demons. We are relying on our own strength. We are stuck in littleness, thinking we have to work harder rather than smarter. We aren't paying attention to the obvious. The door to our future is wide open, and Spirit is tapping us on the shoulder and saying, "Um, excuse me, just turn slightly to the right and walk this way, through the open door," but our response is, sadly: "Oh no, I see this concrete wall over here, I'll just go there. I'm drawn to this wall. If I bang my head against it long enough, it will crack. I can get through with ten or twenty more years of struggle." So many people believe that if they struggle enough, love enough, chip away enough, they can permeate that wall and see the way to their purpose.

Yet all the while, the voice that speaks for God is leading us to the open doorway and life of excitement and joy. In going through that door you'll fulfill your own dreams, and also support a lot of others in fulfilling their dreams. This door is open for you. The way to proceed is so obvious, but we insist on making it so difficult. It really isn't difficult at all. What is making the process so difficult, such a struggle, is our ego, the part of us that does not delight in our breaking through old limitations, that does not support our living in joy. The ego loves struggle and loves to

> The seed of God is within us . . .
> Pear seeds grow into pear trees, nut seeds
> into nut trees and God Seed into God.
>
> ·MEISTER ECKHART·

make life hard and painful and disappointing, and for many it is remarkably successful. The decision can be easy: we need only have a little willingness to leave old behavior patterns behind to seek and find that which is our soul's destiny.

When we are living with purpose, fulfilling our unique divine design, our lives are in order, an order that is often called "divine." To affirm frequently "divine order" may help us in aligning what we are doing with what our purpose is. Affirm hourly, daily, that there is a divine order established in your life—in your work, in your other activities, in your relationships, in your mind, in your body. Here are some helpful affirmations:

My life is now in divine order.

Divine order is now established in my mind, in my body, and in all activities of my life.

Everything out of accord with the divine order of my life I now willingly and easily release. Only that which is for my highest good remains.

When you have a sense that life is becoming too hectic or disconnected, stop and affirm:

Divine order is established here and now.

State this emphatically, with power, conviction, and meaning.

Affirming divine order means realigning all aspects of our lives, bringing them into harmony with all others. It means cleaning out the mental, emotional, and material clutter from your life. I had an acquaintance who was a bibliophile, the owner of thousands of books. She lived in a small apartment with not nearly enough space for her personal library. There were books everywhere. And yet she had her own sense of divine order. There were narrow passageways for her and her guests to walk. As she maneuvered through the tunnels of books, she would gleefully affirm an abbreviated version of divine order. "D.O.! D.O.!" (It was quite comical. It looked like a mess to me, but it seemed to work for her.)

If you have put order in your life, and are experiencing ease, success, fulfillment, and joy, while those around you—family, friends, co-workers—are locked in their own struggle, banging their heads against that concrete wall, what happens to your relationships with these people? Do you give yourself permission to have an easy life when people around you are still mired in their own struggles? Do you feel you are betraying them? If your parents had to sacrifice and struggle to raise you, and you aren't carrying on with that heritage of struggle, does that invalidate their worth, threaten the way they choose to live their lives? This is a dilemma, however confident you may feel with your life. You must release yourself from and forgive all false ideas that come from well-meaning but unenlightened family members, and all limited thoughts and expectations of church, school, and society. This is the only way to discover, awaken to, and embrace your unique divine purpose. Nancy's story is a case in point. *A Course in Miracles* calls all such ideas "upside down," and they truly are an upside-down way of thinking and living your life.

Nancy always believed her purpose was to be a nurse in a hospital. She went to nursing school because that was her mother's dream for her. Nancy's mother had wanted to be a nurse, but she became pregnant with Nancy and married at a

> How could the soul not take flight
> when from the glorious presence
> A soft call flows sweet as honey,
> comes right up to her
> And whispers, "Rise up now, come away."
>
> ·RUMI·

young age, and never attained her goal. The closest she came was to work as one of the "ladies in pink" at a local hospital.

Nancy, an extremely bright and capable young woman, rose quickly to the top in her field. The administrator at the hospital where she worked offered to have the hospital pay Nancy's tuition for evening classes with which she would earn her master's degree. Nancy had to agree that for every year she received tuition payments from the hospital, she would commit to a year of employment with the hospital. Initially she was delighted with the plan, and her mother's pride was overwhelming.

It was quite a challenge for Nancy to balance her work, her studies, and a budding romance with a self-assured, happy young man. The more she pursued her studies, the more dissatisfied she became with her obligation to stay at the hospital for each year spent at school. She was feeling like an indentured servant. But why? she would ask herself. Didn't she love nursing? Wasn't this the fulfillment of her childhood dream? She became increasingly depressed and finally went to a therapist. Nancy came to talk to me after six months of therapy, having come to the realization that it wasn't her dream to be a nurse. It also was not her dream or her desire to go to graduate school—it was her mother's dream and her administrator's desire. Nancy didn't know what she wanted; she had always believed she wanted what her mother had longed for.

I gave Nancy some simple, yet practical and effective, ideas to work with:

1. She needed to give herself permission to live her own life, to discover her own dreams. I had her keep a journal, and record anything and everything that had been or was of interest to her. (Among her interests were riding a horse, reflexology, rock music, healing herbs, and collecting and restoring antique dolls.)
2. She needed to allow herself to leave where she was, and turn and walk through the doors that were open for her.

It took a while, but Nancy dropped out of the master's program. Speaking of the decision several years later, she told me, "It was really scary at the time, but looking back, I see it was one of the best decisions of my life." As Nancy closed the door on a dream that was not hers, other doors began to open. She spent the next fourteen months working sixty hours a week to reimburse the hospital for her schooling, but also—more important—to get a clear idea of who *Nancy* was and what she wanted to do.

During this time Nancy met a famous author and was offered a position as his personal assistant. Since this gentleman was an older man with a few health concerns, he felt very comfortable with Nancy's background as a nurse. Yet he had hired her not as his nurse, but as his spokesperson and coordinator of his busy schedule. Nancy now travels around the world meeting and working with fascinating people; she loves her boss, her new

> There's a divinity that shapes our ends,
> rough hew them how we will.
>
> ·WILLIAM SHAKESPEARE·

career, her new life. She earns three times what she did as a nurse, has a beautiful condominium, and rides her boss's horses several times a week. Nancy has let go of her mother's dream and is now happily living her own.

Here is a way to help you tune in to your divine purpose:

1. Brainstorm a list of everything you like to do, roughly in order of importance to you, the most important activity first. Include anything you enjoy or are good at, whether it's mathematics, science, computers, abstract thinking, mysticism, ocean sports, reading, philosophy, being with the elderly, organizing, or gourmet cooking.
2. Read over your list and put it away for one or two days. Make an appointment with yourself to work further with your list.
3. When you return to your list, reread it, add to it anything that may have occurred to you since you put it away, and review the order of the items. Make sure the activity that appeals to you most is number one, the second most is number two, and so forth. It may surprise you that the order this time may differ from the original order.
4. Examine the top ten items on your list. See whether any of the activities relate to one another. Then close your eyes and let your mind relax. With these activities in

mind, what occurs to you as far as uncovering your divine purpose? If writing, travel, and tennis are in your top ten, for example, perhaps you're meant to be a tennis writer covering tournaments worldwide. Don't limit yourself to just one idea, however. Play with this over a period of time.

5. Once you've decided on something you'd like to pursue, such as being a tennis writer, take action. Subscribe to tennis magazines if you haven't already done so. Write to sports journalists who cover tennis and ask them how they got started; read whatever you can by them. Contact newspapers and magazines and ask what the requirements are for a sportswriting position. Perhaps you'll discover you need more schooling. That's okay—investigate schools. If you are on the track of your divine purpose, everything you do in pursuit of it will inspire and energize you. If you aren't, it will be a struggle and draining. Pay attention to how you feel. Follow your heart. It will lead you into Right Livelihood, your divine purpose.

We all have a creative genius within ourselves, and this genius presents itself only when we are living out our divine purpose. When we are living our mission, we will find helpful people coming forward who act like angels in our lives. This is when we are gently led into the next great opportunity. When this flow of wondrous synchronicity begins, however, we must be careful not to be frightened and sabotage the whole process. I am reminded of what happened to a close friend of mine.

Gordon is a talented photojournalist who has achieved international recognition and earned countless awards for his work.

> The secret of success is constancy to purpose.
>
> ·BENJAMIN DISRAELI·

He now works full-time on a small regional magazine in the Southwest. He and his family live in a town devoid of artistic stimulation. Gordon perpetually reflects on why he stays in such a dismal community; usually he says it's best for his young children and wife to be near her parents and sisters. His work on the magazine is less than stimulating, and certainly not challenging or rewarding.

Meanwhile, Gordon has had offers and opportunities galore from other publications, positions that other photojournalists dream of. After much inner struggle, he has turned them all down. His reputation is ever so slowly eroding by his not accepting these "divine" opportunities. He has buried within himself unresolved fears: fear of breaking the bonds of family, fear of living up to his full potential, fear of being able to deal with international acclaim.

Self-Worth

"Your worth is established by God," *A Course in Miracles* states. Nancy and Gordon, like so many of us, had thought their worth lay in what they did. Her worth was in being a nurse, his in being a sacrificing husband and photojournalist. I used to think my worth was in being a minister. Our worth is not in what we *do,* our worth is who we *are.* When we are in touch, in tune, with who we are, then we are drawn to what we can do that will bring us joy. No price could ever be set on how precious you are to

God. What price, what value, have you been placing on yourself? Not in an egotistical way, but in an "I get it" way. What value do you place on discovering and acknowledging your purpose? It is easy to see that Gordon has a valuable gift to give the world. But he is not seeing it, because he spends endless hours dissipating his power in an inner battle over what he should do.

One of my favorite passages from *A Course in Miracles* is this: "Child of God, you were created to create the good, the beautiful, and the holy." "Child of God" is your true and eternal identity. You are created for a mighty purpose. To recognize if you are living in accord with this mighty purpose, you must ask yourself, "Does my life reflect goodness, beauty, and ease? Am I consciously connecting with the divine? Am I happy?"

My friend Linda and I met on my first Sunday as a minister. We have always felt a unique cosmic connection because that was a first for her too, her first visit to that Unity church. Through the many years I have known her, I have celebrated with her in her journey of dynamic growth in consciousness and dynamic transformation in her outer presence. And it has been an enormous transformation on both counts: Linda rose from a very sickly physical condition into excellent health, and from an emotionally scarred past to a state of forgiveness and freedom.

Ten years ago, with a great deal of skill and a small amount of capital, Linda began her own office systems company. She acquired gorgeous offices, a staff of four, and was so busy she had to turn business away. Despite this success, Linda held a dream of owning or managing a retreat center. Several years ago she learned of an opportunity to work at a retreat conference center in Hawaii for four months, with the possibility of a longer commitment. She did something that to the bottom-line people of the world would appear outrageous: she decided she no longer

> Little minds are tamed and subdued by misfortune; but great minds rise above it.
>
> ·WASHINGTON IRVING·

wanted the responsibility or the stress of being a woman executive. She closed her business; gave away, sold, or put in storage her worldly possessions, including expensive office equipment and fine art; and moved to Hawaii. Some folks thought Linda had gone off the deep end. I thought her decision was one of the most courageous and life-affirming of anyone I had ever known. After she was at the Hawaii center a few weeks, she was offered a permanent position. Here she stayed, living on the campus in simple accommodations just steps from a very dramatic ocean cliff where she would walk each night to watch dolphins play and giant sea turtles coming to feed. By changing her lifestyle, she became radiant, healthy, and happy. Linda literally glowed!

She no longer works at the retreat center—it got to be too much like work. She now lives in a tropical cottage with an organic garden, where she grows produce and herbs that she markets once a week, along with delicious breads and other goodies from her garden and kitchen. Here is a woman who once worked twelve-hour days and wore high heels and suits every day; now she tills the earth, bakes whole-grain breads, and goes to market once a week wearing a colorful sarong. She is sharing goodness and nourishment, and is connected with the divine.

Linda had to rid herself of her emotional baggage to get to that inner radiant love, and now she shares her bounty through her gardening and baking and, most important, through her consciousness of love, which she shares freely with others.

We are all guided as to what to do next. Linda listened and followed. Gordon listens and considers his options, discounts himself, struggles, and remains stuck. Linda is happy. Gordon is not.

Linda walked through the door that was open. When we walk through the door that is open, the first space we enter may not be the fulfillment of our dream. It may be only the vestibule, yet we may enter and become comfortable and successful there. In time, we may look around again and see another door opening. This is a continual process as we move into ever-expanding spheres of good. This is so different from insisting on doing it on our own, and the only results are limited degree of satisfaction and great degree of struggle and sacrifice. When we enter the welcoming space on the other side of the open door, we cease struggling to make something work. Here we are in tune with our divine purpose—to be happy, to create the good, the beautiful, and the holy. Here we experience an easy and orderly flow, and our good goes before us to create even greater good. Here we "live with the license of a higher order of beings."

It's up to you to open yourself to what could be possible for you. What is the desire of your heart that is in alignment with your divine purpose?

Keeping a Journal

For several weeks keep a journal of what gives you a sense of inner fullness, what brings you into a state of ease and comfort. Write in the journal for twenty minutes the first thing every morning. Don't think of what you write as needing to relate to your career, just write what makes you happy. Remember Nancy, who listed among her interests horseback riding and healing herbs? What lies buried within you?

> To will what God wills is the only science that gives us rest.
>
> ·HENRY WADSWORTH LONGFELLOW·

Take some quiet time to work with this exercise. Place yourself in a light state of relaxation by breathing deeply several times, closing your eyes, and releasing tension, stress, and strain. Breathe them out. When you are relaxed, ask your inner divine self:

What is my divine purpose?

What would God have me do to bring me joy, fulfillment, and financial ease?

What is my right livelihood?

How may I make a contribution?

What am I to do for my good and the good of all?

Ask for guidance and it will be given to you. Be sure to write every idea and thought that comes to you. Do not discount or disregard any idea as silly, unimportant, or without value. In time any thought lacking value will be edited out. For now write them all on paper. When a theme begins to emerge, do *some* outer activity that is supportive of that inner idea. One of the ideas I had on my list was writing. When I first had the desire to communicate through the written word, and no longer just the spoken word, I enrolled in creative writing courses, where I received support and encouragement from instructors and classmates. I studied how to write and get magazine articles published. Initially, I could envision myself writing and successfully selling articles to magazine. It took a year for my consciousness to expand sufficiently for me to consider writing not just articles on conscious relationships, but my first book, *A Course in Love.*

When guidance comes, it gently instructs us what the next step should be. A few years ago I could see the value of taking a writing course. I was not able then to conceive of what was to follow.

Right now doors are opening for you. Right now the way is being made clear. You are free to make a choice. You are free to walk through the door that is open, and you can walk into your good. You can walk toward the light as it comes forward to greet you, saying, "Welcome, welcome home."

It takes a person who is wide-awake to have his dreams come true.

ANONYMOUS

My life is focused on having my dreams come true, and they always do. Let's you and I dream the happy dream together.

I learned this, at least, by my experiment; that if one advances confidently in the direction of his dreams, and endeavors to live the life which he has imagined, he will meet with a success unexpected in common hours. He will put some things behind, will pass an invisible boundary; new, universal, and more liberal laws will begin to establish themselves around and within him; or the old laws will be expanded, and interpreted in his favor in a more liberal sense, and he will live with the license of a higher order of beings.

·HENRY DAVID THOREAU·

Life Is Consciousness

The Spiritual Law of Consciousness 3

When I was in my first year of ministerial school, the senior students would frequently greet any and every plight, complaint, or triumph of their underclassmates with the clipped and compassionless phrase: *"Life is consciousness!"*

When I heard this principle repeated, my heart was rarely comforted, and often unsettled. It wasn't until much later that I realized that the laws of Spirit do not coddle us, or make allowances for our ignorance of their exacting ways. I eventually understood why the seniors repeated this primary law of being without couching its sting or absolute truth.

If we can understand just this one fundamental law of living, we can live radically transformed lives. This Spiritual Principle is my personal favorite, because it teaches us not only that we are in charge, but that we can at any moment change the outer picture we see. Of course we have to believe this, but our belief in the law does not alter its being the law. Consciousness is the sum total of all our thoughts and feelings.

> Your own self-realization is the greatest service you can render the world.
>
> ·SRI ROMANA MAHARISHI·

Thoughts + Feelings = Consciousness

The world is not what it appears to be. We perceive the world according to our consciousness. It is for you what it appears to be to you. That does not mean it is actually that way. It exists that way only in your consciousness.

To achieve any given desire, ideal, or goal, the consciousness for it must be established within you. Without question you must know that you are deserving, worthy, and ready, welcoming the state of mind or the thing desired.

Many years ago a metaphysical teacher, Emmett Fox, presented the classic idea of the "mental equivalent," namely, that to achieve a goal or desire, you must first create its mental equivalent. (This is simply another way to express the idea that life is consciousness.) You must first create the mental equivalent of a healthy body if your desire is for greater physical health. You must first create the mental equivalent of a holy relationship if your desire is to attract your ideal partner. You must first create the mental equivalent of a career advancement if your desire is to move into a higher position.

The building of consciousness is a divine activity. Here you are rising and joining with God as co-creator—specifically the co-creator of your life and desired good. Let's look at this teaching through an example.

Take Susan. Say her predominant thoughts about her career,

superiors, and colleagues in her consciousness are: "They only want to suck the lifeblood out of me. Companies don't care about their employees. All the people here are cutthroats, only out for themselves. I can't trust anyone, let alone the organization." Susan is filled with anger, fear, and resentment. She fears for her future, is angry or disillusioned with co-workers, and feels victimized by other people's actions or nonactions.

These thoughts added to these feelings *have* to result in her constantly reenacting the same unsatisfying, miserable scene. Even if she changes companies, her experiences would be no different from what they were before, because her consciousness is no different from what it was before.

If she wants to change her circumstances, Susan must change her thoughts about bosses, colleagues, work environment, and so on. She needs to recognize her fear, anger, and hostility, and then be willing to release them. She needs to learn to experience peace instead of constant turmoil, to feel contentment for her work rather than rage, to adopt a sense of caring and compassion for her superiors and colleagues rather than see them as enemies; she needs to see them as people like her, doing their very best.

Susan would, mindfully and systematically, have to replace every sense of fear and anger with love. Only when her inner world changes can her outer world change. This is true for all of us: once we wake up and realize that "life is consciousness," we can begin to expand our individual expression of consciousness and move toward our greatest desires.

The Universal Law of Mind Action is: "Thoughts held in mind produce after their kind." Just as apple seeds produce apple trees and tomato seeds produce tomato plants, so too do thoughts we plant in our minds produce after their kind. You don't plant cactus seeds and expect to produce a gardenia. Nor

> Therefore . . . be ye lamps unto yourself, be ye a refuge to yourself. Betake yourself to no external refuge. Hold fast to the Truth as a lamp; hold fast to the Truth as a refuge. Look not for a refuge in anyone beside yourself.
>
> ·THE BUDDHA·

do you plant seeds of bitterness and expect to produce loving kindness. Our thoughts are seeds that we are always planting, and the day of harvest is always at hand.

The Dhammapada tells us, "All that we are is the result of all that we have thought." Another way of putting it is: We are what we think about all day long.

Honestly examine your thinking. What kinds of seeds have you been sowing? What do you think about all day long? Do you think kind, loving, abundant thoughts, or do you think resentful, hurtful, stingy thoughts? Whatever is occupying your mind, you are going to reap the same.

Look at your life today. What do you have before you and within you? If it's beautiful and desirable, it's because beautiful and desirable thoughts have been planted in the past in your mind. If your life is less than desirable, the cause is the undesirable thoughts that have been planted in your fertile consciousness. A peaceful perception of the world can arrive only from a peaceful mind. A peaceful mind can result only from the consistent planting of thoughts of peace.

I recall Thich Nhat Hanh's words of wisdom about many peace activists during the Vietnam War. He felt that they could not be very effective in facilitating peace because they had so many internal warlike thoughts themselves. They could write scathing protest letters, but were unable to write effective love letters.

Thoughts held in mind produce after their kind. Hold angry, warlike thoughts in mind and they produce warlike experiences. Hold holy, peaceful thoughts in mind and they produce peaceful experiences, and a peaceful world for you. A peaceful mind knows God. The memory of God returns to a mind at peace. The memory of God cannot come where there is conflict. A mind at war against itself cannot remember eternal gentleness.

If you're browsing through *Architectural Digest* and you see the home of your dreams, and your first thought is, "I'll never have a home as splendid as that," you're absolutely right. If your gut feeling is resentment or envy of the "rich people who live there," your self-created destiny of being a have-not is cemented in place.

But when you awaken to the glorious life you could have and are fully engaged with God as your co-creator, your first thought is, "What a splendid house!" You might cut the picture out of the magazine and tape it to your refrigerator door, and every morning you look at it and breathe in all that it means to you. You feel worthy to live in such a beautiful home. Your thoughts and feelings are developing within you the consciousness that will one day enable you to have a home like that—or one even better.

When we live with the understanding that life is consciousness, we can deal with *cause,* and we can change and adjust and transform. When we are ignorant of this Spiritual Principle, we deal with outer effects only. And no matter how much we manipulate outer effects, our situation isn't going to change permanently. Manipulating effects has been described as trying to stop

> Believe nothing because a wise man said it.
> Believe nothing because it is generally held.
> Believe nothing because it is written.
> Believe nothing because it is said to be divine.
> Believe nothing because someone else believes it.
> But believe only what you yourself judge to be true.
>
> ·THE BUDDHA·

the sinking of the *Titanic* by rearranging the deck chairs: if the starboard chairs are just moved to the port side, then everything will be okay.

A skilled means to recognize where our individual consciousness abides is to observe ourselves from another person's viewpoint, that is, do as Strickland Gillilan wrote: "Just stand aside and watch yourself go by, Think of yourself as 'he' instead of 'I.' "

The superb news about consciousness is that it is not set in stone. It is not predetermined. It is malleable. It can grow, expand, and change. It can be transformed.

As the inner consciousness grows, expands, changes, and is transformed, so too does your life and its outer picture. Consciousness is the result of years of development, and the cause of all effect.

In my first book, *A Course in Love,* I wrote extensively of my journey out of the pain, sadness, and anger of my early relationships, and into the holy relationship with my beloved, to whom I've been married for ten years. The transformation from pain into bliss has been the result of first recognizing where my consciousness had been abiding, and next clearing and expanding my consciousness to accept more and more of the divine plan into my life. I had to develop the consciousness that said:

Yes, I am deserving.

Yes, this kind of love is possible.

No, I will no longer accept crumbs and call them love.

Yes, God wants me to live in love.

Yes, this is possible—not only possible but spiritually true.

Following is the greatest story I know of a woman's overcoming horrendous experiences and using them as a catalyst to heal her soul and create a consciousness of remarkable clarity.

My precious friend Linda and I met in ministerial school. We were students together for one overlapping year, my first and her last. It could not be said back then that we were friends, more like acquaintances. Linda appeared warm, compassionate, protected . . . and sad, and those same words could have been applied to me. We were similar on a soul level, although the causes of the warmth, compassion, protection, and sadness came out of very different life experiences.

Linda was the only child of parents who divorced when she was two, and Linda's life was thereafter void of paternal love. This darling child was left with a void that grew only larger as she got older. When she was five, her mother married a man thirty years her senior. It seemed that Linda at long last had her "daddy." She and her mother had someone who loved them and would care for them. They would have a home and a family.

They lived in a remote rural area of the Northwest. Linda attended a tiny public school, and her mother and stepfather operated a motel, the only one in the region. The family quarters were attached to one end of the motel, and Linda did after-school and weekend chores to help the business. As she moved into her preteen years, her stepfather expanded her responsibil-

> Spiritual life is the bouquet, the perfume,
> the flowering and fulfillment of a human life,
> not a supernatural virtue imposed on it.
>
> ·JOSEPH CAMPBELL·

ities. At night, while her mother would be at the front desk, at the far end of the motel, her stepfather would creep into Linda's room and, without a word, rape her. Afterward he would threaten her with the greatest fear: If she told anyone, *she* would be responsible for destroying their "family." She would no longer have a family. She and her mother would no longer have a home.

Night after terrifying night, this bright and beautiful child endured unspeakable horrors and abuse. Her light began to dim, her spirit retreated, and she became numb, not only to what was occurring in her life but to life itself. She shut down mentally and emotionally and in her consciousness moved as far away as possible from this personal horror. The torturous conditions continued until Linda was sixteen and a senior in high school. The fateful day came when she had the courage to say, *"No! No more!"*

She was planning to go with several friends to a football game in a neighboring town. Before leaving, she had to pull the weeds in the flower beds around the motel. When she had finished she went to tell her stepfather she was leaving for the game. He replied that he had one more job for her: to have oral sex with him.

Linda, now healed, says she does not know what was different about that day more than thirty years ago, why her stepfather's additional dehumanizing demand triggered the resolve for her to stand up to him and say, *"No!"*

After enduring years of sexual and emotional abuse, she was finally able to say to him, "I don't care what privileges you withhold from me, what your threats may be, what happens between my mother and you, but you will never, ever touch my body again!" And he did not. But the wounds of his abuse bore through Linda's flesh and into her soul.

Later, Linda married young and had a son, whom she loves deeply. The marriage was not right for her. She could not be fully present with her husband, and she built a stronger barrier around herself in a desperate attempt to protect herself from her unhealed pain.

About twelve years ago Linda and I attended the same winter conference, and we went out to dinner one evening. She mentioned that I seemed much clearer, happier, and freer than when we were in school. What was I doing?

I shared some of my experiences with therapy and described the breath work I had been doing. She expressed interest in doing the breath work and asked whether I would work with her. She was willing to drive the ten hours to my home to do this deep soul-healing work.

I agreed to the plan, but she still seemed hesitant. After a pause she said that I had to know something about her and be comfortable with it in order to do work on such a deep level. I couldn't imagine what it was. She looked me in the eyes and blurted out, "I am a lesbian."

"Uh-huh." I nodded.

"You knew?"

"Well, Linda," I responded, "I haven't given it much conscious thought, but yes, I knew."

> Whoever knows the All but fails
> to know himself lacks everything.
>
> ·GOSPEL ACCORDING TO THOMAS·

After I learned her story, I would have been astonished if she had not been a lesbian. Not that sexual abuse turns every young girl into a lesbian. But one does not have to be a psychiatrist to conclude that sex with any man after the horror she had experienced would not be a very inviting proposition.

I tell you Linda's story in such detail so that you can grasp the full impact of what I now write.

Linda is among the most alive, healed conscious beings I know. During her remarkable soul journey of the past dozen years she has explored every available avenue to healing with total resolve, just as total as the resolve she showed that fateful day when she first defied her stepfather and said, *"No!"*

Linda has worked on cleansing her consciousness, on healing every one of her memories—memories locked not just in her mind but in the cells of her physical body as well. She has screamed and pounded, raged and sobbed. She wrote in her journal, and spent years in group and individual counseling. She traveled to the cellular level of her own being and with the grace of God healed her soul, her mind, her body. Through prayer work and forgiveness techniques, Linda was able to create a field of consciousness for a total healing to take place.

Linda first created the consciousness that said yes to the possibility of being actually healed of such horror. Then she moved out of her story of past abuse and out of a history of less than fulfilling relationships with women to open herself up to her perfect partner, whoever God would have that be. At that stage she had the affirmations in place that said:

I am deserving.
I am desirable.
I have a right to be happy.
I deserve true, holy love.

Her feeling nature mirrored her thoughts. She is now a holy woman, no longer a woman filled with holes. Her thoughts and feelings are now in alignment with God's highest good for her. Her entire demeanor and style are transformed: she radiates composure, beauty, love, and the deep compassion that looks at another in pain and silently says, "I know what you are going through. I truly do. And I know it's possible to get through whatever it is and be healed and free."

Because of Linda's experiences and her ensuing healing, she can inspire and guide many wounded individuals on their own spiritual journeys and soul transformations. She is like the mythical phoenix, rising to new life out of the ashes of its old life. May Linda's story inspire you to realize that the healing one dear soul has achieved can be achieved by all who desire the same.

Your present consciousness is the sum of all your current ideas, thoughts, words, feelings, and emotions. This product is the field out of which your current life is being created, moment by moment.

Perhaps you have heard the teaching, "Change your thoughts, change your life." This is true to a degree, but to effect lasting change, more than our thoughts must change. We also must become aware of what prompted the thought, or the thought beneath thought, and alter that subconscious thought. We must watch our conversations, which reflect our thoughts,

> He who sees that the Lord of all is ever the same in all that is, immortal in the field of mortality—
> he sees the truth.
> And when a man sees that the God in himself is the same God in all that is, he hurts not himself by hurting others; then he goes indeed to the highest path.
>
> ·BHAGAVAD GITA·

and hold fast to what we know to be true in our hearts and innermost being.

Transformation of consciousness is much more than simple change. On one level it is a metamorphosis of one's entire being and view of life. The nature of life itself not only calls us to move into the deepest levels of being and live from our true center, but demands this of us. When we ignore the call, our lives become more and more painful and difficult. We become ensnared in the difficulties, and live out of the ensuing negativity.

In these circumstances, we may feel desperate, but we are not without hope. For no matter how far off course we may be, there is always a way back and out and up. Perhaps you have seen those bumper stickers that read SHIT HAPPENS. I recall seeing that message for the first time and saying to myself: "Now there's a negative thinker if ever I've seen one." But there are other messages, just as strong. A friend of mine showed up one day with a T-shirt that stated boldly TRANSFORMATION HAPPENS. Recently I saw one that said GRACE HAPPENS, and a bumper sticker that read MAGIC HAPPENS.

The transformation of consciousness from negativity and pain is grace in action. It is crucial to understand the importance of our consciousness is spiritual growth. Our consciousness expands and grows as our individual "me-ness" comes into perfect alignment with our Godness, but this can occur only if we are vigilant to drop limited, negative ways and beliefs and embrace our divine potential. If we do we are truly transforming our consciousness.

Life is the direct result of our consciousness: this spiritual principle supports every level of being and must be applied to all circumstances of body and soul.

The following exercise may assist you in distinguishing between what your inner consciousness determines to be true and what you are currently experiencing.

An Exercise in Consciousness

On a sheet of paper make headings for two columns, and label them A and B. In Column A, list what you hold in your mind to be true, including your inner feelings. Be honest. In Column B, list what you desire to experience as true, along with how you would feel. For example:

Column A	Column B
I count every penny. I never donate to any charity because I don't have the extra money.	I desire financial ease and security.
I gossip about my friends and co-workers.	I desire kind, loving, supportive friends.
I am quick-tempered and brood over every slight.	I desire a quiet mind and peace.

I feel misunderstood.	I desire to be understood for who I really am.
I am easily hurt and feel nervous, scared, vulnerable.	I have a clear sense of self. I desire to feel at ease, confident, secure in various situations.

Now make your own list.

The expansion of consciousness occurs as we awaken to realize we are creating our moment-to-moment reality ourselves. If we do not enjoy the outer picture (column A), we can change it by realigning our thoughts, feelings, attitudes, and conversations. A positive shift within must result in a positive shift without. This is a spiritual law, a divine principle. We must clear our consciousness and elevate our sense of worthiness.

It is beneficial to write out affirmations such as these below. (Write your name in the blanks, in this and all the exercises.)

It's safe for me, ____________, to open up and be free.
It's safe for me, ____________, to change.
It's safe for me, ____________, to do new things.
It's safe for me, ____________, to give to others.
It's safe for me, ____________, to have new experiences.
It's safe for me, ____________, to release my anger.
It's safe for me, ____________, to find new pleasures.
I, ____________, deserve to have an open, free life now.
I, ____________, deserve to have a changed life now.
I, ____________, deserve to have greater financial ease.
I, ____________, deserve to have loving, supportive friends.

I, ____________, deserve to have new pleasures.
I, ____________, deserve to have a quiet mind.

Further affirmations to help you along in this process:

My life is becoming more open and free.

Every day, in every way, my life is changing for the better.

I now delight in new experiences and find great pleasure in each day.

My outer world is in perfect harmony with my inner world.

I am fully integrated in my inner and outer life.

As above, so below.

As within, so without.

Spiritual principles teach us that we can have anything we truly want. We can be anything we truly desire. We can attract anything we truly set our heart and mind upon. Linda's case is extreme; I use it to make this point: If the most horrific abuse can be healed, so too can your situation. She now has a relationship with a partner, a home, a healed relationship with her mother, a career, all the things she ever wanted, and most important, she has been healed of her childhood trauma. Her pain is no longer the creative energy of her life, and her soul twinkles with light and love.

And to have all the things she wanted, to have a life of light

> The more noble and excellent the soul is,
> the greater and more savory are its perceptions.
>
> ·JEREMY TAYLOR·

> All who know their own minds,
> do not know their own hearts.
>
> ·FRANÇOIS DE LA ROCHEFOUCAULD·

and love, she had first to create the consciousness of it within. Likewise, we must all first create the consciousness within for anything we want in order to have it in our outer reality. Years ago, Dr. Maxwell Maltz, a noted plastic surgeon, discovered this teaching to be true as he transformed disfigured facial features and found his patients still carrying the internal wounds of their outer disfigurements. They did not have the inner consciousness in alignment with their new outer beauty. They still saw themselves as scarred and disfigured.

It is a delight to share with you one of my very best demonstrations of spiritual principle, of building the consciousness of a desired good. My husband and I live in a lovely condominium near Lake Erie, on a large expanse of manicured land. Before purchasing our unit, we leased another in the same building for five years. David and I loved our home and wanted to stay, but the owner had put it up for sale, and we were not in a financial position to buy it. We began looking elsewhere to rent. We explored every possibility we knew of in a twenty-five-mile radius. Nothing felt quite right. What we really wanted to do was stay in the same building, but rents had escalated so much in those five years that we could no longer afford to lease any of the few available units.

We knew there was a perfect home for us, and we began affirming and praying daily for it. We opened ourselves to whatever was for our greater good, and we spoke only in positive terms as we pursued every lead that came our way. Then one day I recalled a woman we had met when we first moved in. She no longer lived in her unit, and her tenants had left to buy their own unit. I tracked her down and found out that her unit was not only vacant, but had been so for almost a year.

When I called, I assumed she would rather accept a bit less than the going rental rate than the nothing she was currently getting. In our initial conversation she was open to my proposal, but she said what she really wanted to do was to sell the unit. She wanted to speak to her husband, she told me, and would call back.

David and I kept up our inner knowing, affirming that we deserved a lovely home, one that was affordable, conveniently located, and appropriate to our busy lives.

When the woman phoned, she brought forth an offer better than anything we had dreamed of. She and her husband wanted to sell the unit, she said. So what if they held the mortgage for five years and we bought it with $10,000 down? It sounded great to us, but we didn't have the $10,000 to put down, and I told her so.

What she proposed next happily stunned us. "Okay then, what if we hold the mortgage for five years and you put nothing down?" I shook my head to clear my ears. Was I hearing correctly? Nothing down?

Several days later the four of us met and worked out the details with the help of an attorney friend. There was a plan for us which was for our highest good, and it far exceeded our expectations. We had opened our united consciousness to know that we were deserving, that something perfect would work out, and we remained available to whatever that was to be.

Our collective consciousness attracted an almost unbeliev-

> Each heart is a world. You find all within yourself that you find without.
>
> ·JOHN CASPAR LAVATER·

able solution to our dwelling dilemma. At that time it would have been inconceivable to me that we could pay off the balance in full. But my consciousness of abundance has expanded, and that is exactly what is happening.

Whatever it is that you desire—from a healed soul to a perfect home, from a new face to a new car—inwardly develop the consciousness for it, and it shall be yours. Practice the following:

1. Clear and develop your consciousness by replacing negative, false thoughts with positive, spiritual, true ones.
2. Through meditation and quiet reflection, move into the subconscious realm and plant the seed thoughts of your worthiness.
3. Hold a constant image in mind of the desired state of affairs.
4. Release any image that creeps into your consciousness and conflicts with the new image.
5. Do your spiritual work to be healed on an emotional level. Release to the Holy Spirit all negative emotions.
6. Tune in to the one true spiritual feeling, which is love, and live from love, blessing all people, situations, animals, and things with love.

As you continue with this practice, your consciousness will rise to embrace your greater good, and you shall continue to draw forth from God's limitless reservoir your personal blessing of good. You can learn to "express reality there if you wish," to quote Richard Bach.

Wherever you are, the reality of your spiritual nature will be expressed there. This Spiritual Principle may become your constant companion, as it is for those who go about co-creating daily lives of remarkable splendor. Remember, it is always necessary to create first within our thoughts and feelings the equivalent of whatever we desire. The principle of consciousness covers all other spiritual principles. A deep and clear understanding of this Universal Law will always serve you well. Never forget: *Life is consciousness!*

The Blind Can See

The Spiritual Law of Vision

4

The brilliant singer and songwriter Karen Karsh sings, "If you could see the way I see it, hear what I hear, see the world through my eyes, listen with my ears, then the world would be different. It wouldn't be the same. Come on and see the way I do, everything would change."

Karen is a beautiful woman, goddesslike, with a mane of flowing black hair. She has a huge laugh, and vibrates enough energy to fill a concert hall; her heart radiates unabashed joy. She is candid, outrageously funny . . . and blind since birth, as a result of a horrendous miscalculation in the administration of oxygen at her premature delivery. Without the use of her eyes, Karen sees in a way most people never even touch.

As I'm writing, I am ensconced in my favorite spot, watching dawn break over an extremely calm Pacific Ocean. The gray-blue clouds turn a golden pink with a halo of white. The ocean is all shades of soft blue, with reflections of the pink clouds rippling

> Because you cannot see me with your own natural eye,
> I will give you a celestial eye.
>
> ·BHAGAVAD GITA·

across the surface with remarkable beauty. And I think, What if I could not see the swaying palms or the plumeria in bloom? What if I couldn't see the day awakening?

My spiritual studies have taught me that true seeing does not come with the physical eyes. Often what the physical eyes perceive is a very limited glimpse of reality. Sometimes it's a glimpse into the magnificent, but at other times it's a glimpse into the worst of human conditions. Our physical eyes give us a limited view of reality. It is the awakening of our inner sight that can truly reveal reality to us. Karen Karsh views the world with *insight* because, although her eyes are not capable of seeing, her heart, soul, and spirit have crystal-clear vision. She can see a higher reality because her physical eyes do not deceive her, as ours so often deceive us. She has accessed the "celestial eyes."

This chapter explores how we, sighted and sightless, can move toward true vision and begin to see what is truly possible for each of us. Seeing is of our physical reality, vision is of the spiritual reality. Vision is perceiving God and embracing the spirit. *A Course in Miracles* reminds us that "vision is freely given to those who ask to see." If we are faithful and diligent, as we align ourselves with this inner seeing, our nightmares of a painful, separating reality begin to be transformed into happy dreams of beauty, love, and gentleness.

Again from *A Course in Miracles:* "Vision sets all things right, bringing them gently within the kindly sway of Heaven's law."

Until we awaken to the broader, gentler spiritual reality, we truly believe that the picture our physical eyes sends to us is the totality of possibilities.

In *The Varieties of Religious Experience,* William James warns that when we dwell in such a state of mind that "other potential realities are right there before us veiled by the flimsiest of screens," we risk a great loss, namely that "we may go through life not aware of their existence."

As we move forward on our journey of awakening to their existence, our old patterns of seeing and perceiving must drop away. We begin to understand we are always "seeing" only our view, which is always limited, and filled with past experiences of seeing particular people, objects, or situations. When you see a sibling or an old friend, for example, you are not "seeing" that person fully as he or she is today. Instead, you are experiencing your numerous past encounters with this person you believe you know so well. There is a story of a king from ages past who said that his tailor was the most intelligent man he knew, because each time the tailor came to call, he remeasured the king for his regal garments. We too would be very wise if each time we called on a friend or acquaintance we remeasured them in our minds, to see them as they are in that moment, at that new encounter.

Earth's crammed with heaven,
And every common bush afire with God;
But only he who sees, takes off his shoes,
The rest sit round it and pluck blackberries.

·ELIZABETH BARRETT BROWNING·

A Place to Begin

What we see, behold, claim as reality at any given moment is not actually Reality, but is our individual perception of reality. This individual perception may or may not be aligned with Reality. When we are entrenched in our limited view and equally limited belief system, we cannot even conceive of alternative realities. In order to initiate the shift from where we have been to a gentler place, we need to open our consciousness to say, "Okay, maybe what I see isn't *Reality,* but is only my perception of what is real based on some very limited information." Transformed perception does lead to seeing into a higher Reality.

There is an old story of a much-loved entertainer, now deceased, who would not rest until he found a coin, every single day of his life. Wherever he went, he would look at the pavement in search of his "lucky penny." When we go through life always looking down, our perceptions can be shaded and dark. We may find our lucky coin, but at what cost? Conversely, if we learn through practice and persistence to elevate our point of view, our perception of reality elevates as well, and what we then begin to see is priceless.

In Eastern meditation, practitioners are taught to lift their inner gaze while the eyes are closed. While meditating, they are to focus softly on the center of the forehead, or the third eye. Lifting the inner meditative gaze symbolizes lifting all aspects of

> Progress will be carried forward
> by a series of dazzling visions.
>
> ·VICTOR HUGO·

life to a higher level. It is believed too that such a focus stimulates the pineal gland to release a hormone that leads to deep peace and insightful states of mind. When such meditative techniques are practiced over a period of time, one may see with an inner eye bright lights, symbols, or other ecstatic images. While these visions may occur, while they may be fascinating and reveal another view of reality, it is not wise to make these "light shows" the purpose of meditation. Staying attached to them can detain spiritual progress. Although they are fun and exciting, they are only a possible step on the path, and not the goal of meditative practice.

In my early years as a student of *A Course in Miracles,* I was practicing a daily lesson: "I am determined to see." Countless times one day I silently affirmed this, to every encounter, to every activity I affirmed, "I am determined to see." Late that afternoon, in a burst of energy, I began to "see" a band of blazing golden-white light around everyone I met. These bands appeared around my ministerial school classmates, my instructors, the office personnel, and people in my apartment building. It was a remarkable experience, and though I did not see a "full aura," I was seeing everyone differently. I can still feel the excitement of that personal breakthrough, of seeing a different reality, another possibility. The next day the lesson I practiced was: "I am determined to see things differently." Not only was I determined, I already *was* seeing things differently!

One day a friend and I were in a store checkout line, waiting our turn with a harried and grumpy clerk. I told Betty that we had better start seeing her differently, beyond the harried, grumpy exterior, or we were going to have an unpleasant encounter. So right there in line we affirmed softly, "God, I am determined to see this child of yours and sister of ours differently." By the time we were in front of her we could see her bright spiritual side and not the sullen mask. We left the checkout line smiling and wishing one another a great day.

I have observed, in years of practicing this and similar spiritual ideas, that not only my world has transformed and become more peaceful, but where I am physically and what my eyes see become more and more beautiful. Real vision allows us to see beyond the appearance of harried grumpiness into someone's beautiful spirit. Vision allows us to see the spiritual truth of all things that lies beneath the mask, what William James called the "flimsiest of screens." To move beyond seeing with just your physical eyes, to begin to see with your spiritual eyes, you might try this gentle yet powerful technique.

Spiritual Seeing

Find a quiet spot where you will be undisturbed for fifteen minutes. Sit quietly, relax your body, close your eyes, and focus your awareness on the rising and falling of your breath for several counts. After you feel a sense of peace and relaxation, you then begin to practice this lovely, ancient technique.

Now lift the focus of your eyes, still closed, from beneath their lids. Slowly, mindfully, draw the focus to the center of your

> I am convinced that every human being is capable of catching a vision of the transhuman presence and of entering into communion with It.
>
> ·A. J. TOYNBEE·

forehead. In other words, you are now looking at the center of your forehead through closed eyes.

While keeping this focus, with the index and middle finger of one hand softly and slowly circle the spot in the center of your forehead; this can be helpful in awakening the inner light. Do this for one or two minutes, but no more than five. Then rest and move to wherever the meditation leads you. If you are progressing well, you may repeat the circling of the third eye a second or even a third time. When the Light comes, your inner vision will awaken. This is an excellent time to declare that you are determined to see particular people, things, or situations differently. Practice one day with the thought "I am determined to see." Follow the next day with the thought "I am determined to see differently." When you feel you are seeing differently, expand the exercise to include one or more of the following during your meditations:

> I am determined to see myself differently from how I saw myself in the past.
>
> I am determined to see myself differently from how I see my mother.
>
> I am determined to see myself differently from how I see my father.
>
> I am determined to see my spouse differently.
>
> I am determined to see my best friend differently from how I saw him/her ten years ago.
>
> I am determined to see my co-workers differently.
>
> I am determined to see myself differently in regard to finances.

I am determined to see myself differently in regard to opportunities.

I am determined to see myself differently in regard to my physical being.

Faithfully practicing this technique will lead to great shifts in consciousness.

In *A Course in Love,* I taught that what we focus on expands. When the entire focus of our seeing is elevated to the transformation point of true vision, this spiritual law of expansion results in the perpetual increase of all that is gentle, good, successful, joyous, loving, and abundant. As our spiritual vision expands, all of our life ascends into higher levels of awareness, blessings, and joy.

I found a prayer in *A Course in Miracles* so helpful that I copied it on a small card and carried it with me wherever I went; I placed another copy in a prominent place at home so I would remember to repeat it frequently:

I am responsible for what I see.
I choose the feelings I experience and
I decide upon the good I would achieve.
And everything that seems to happen to me
I ask for, and receive as I have asked.

> Imagination rules the world.
>
> ·NAPOLEON BONAPARTE·

> The soul without imagination is what an observatory would be like without a telescope.
>
> ·HENRY WARD BEECHER·

When we learn to take responsibility for what we see, we can begin to transform our seeing. This process of transformation will lead to the spiritualization of our vision, which leads to the spiritualization of our experiences in the world. Life does not happen to us, no matter how long and hard we argue that it does. Remember that ultimate negative bumper sticker, SHIT HAPPENS? Of course it happens, when that is what we are expecting. And when it does happen, in our most negative state we say, "See, shit does happen. And everything that seems to happen, I ask for." We have a remarkable power to create our view of reality; we are the ones who determine if it's a dark world, or one filled with light and love.

"As he thinketh in his heart, so is he," the Book of Proverbs says. Spiritual vision lifts the veil of individual perception and shows us a healed world, a holy world. This doesn't just happen, it is an inner choice we make, a choice we make every day.

I prize this lesson from *A Course in Miracles:* "God is in everything I see because God is in my mind." The clearer our minds become, the easier it is to gain access to the God presence that has forever been there. We see with a clearer perception, and with spiritual eyes. What we see—the pure, the innocent, the beautiful—is what we have returned to. This ancient—yet new—way of seeing is our reality, even in the most trying of circumstances.

This past year I have become very close friends with a young

> Imagination is the eye of the soul.
>
> ·JOSEPH JOUBERT·

Tibetan Buddhist lama, who embodies wisdom and innocence and purity. We have a holy relationship that transcends our different cultures, ages, and backgrounds. Lama Chonam observes that "we must have very good karma together." I just smile, and no longer question being pals with a monk who's always bowing to me and every person he encounters.

Recently Lama Chonam decided to return to his native Tibet to visit his family. This had all the appearances of being an extremely dangerous journey, since the Chinese Communists, who overran his country almost four decades ago, have executed more than a million Tibetans, including tens of thousands of Buddhist monks. Lama Chonam himself escaped four years ago with his cousin, fleeing on foot over the Himalayas and barely surviving the hunger and extreme weather conditions.

I understood his need to return—he had not seen his parents or twelve brothers and sisters in four years—but I had serious concern for his well-being. He told me he would be traveling in ordinary clothes, not in his monk's robes. His route would take him through mainland China, where he would travel four days by bus before encountering Chinese Communist guards at the border with Tibet. I asked my congregation and all my friends to join me in praying for this his safety throughout his trek.

He was supposed to be away one month, and he promised he would call me as soon as he returned. Five, six, seven weeks went by, and no phone call. I continued praying for his safety, many times each day. Deep inside, however, I felt that he was well and safe. And after two full months the phone call came. He was back . . . and safe. He told me his story.

At the border, his two traveling companions, both monks, were questioned by the guards and quickly passed through. Then it was his turn, and one of the first questions he was asked was, "Are you a monk?"

Lama Chonam immediately told the truth, "Yes, I am." What followed were four hours of intensive, nonstop interrogation by several guards. Many questions were asked about the Dalai Lama, including what Lama Chonam felt about His Holiness. Under these most challenging of circumstances, he responded with total candor and innocence, "I love the Dalai Lama very much."

As Lama Chonam related his experiences to me, I asked him, "Were you afraid?"

He paused for a long time and finally, with some surprise at my question, said in his soft, peaceful voice, "Afraid? No, I was not afraid." He then told me that upon leaving he had been given papers to assure him immediate reentry into his country on all future trips.

The circumstances of his visit sounded very frightening to me, but this man of Spirit never entertained the idea of fear. He lives in inner peace, maintains his inner vision, regardless of the outer picture of life. Lama Chonam obviously sees all things differently.

Making a Treasure Map—A Pictured Prayer

A powerful technique to support us in seeing our world differently and consciously creating what we want is to make a Treasure Map, an outer picture of our inner prayers and desires. This can be a creative, even fun, project.

> All I have seen teaches me to trust the Creator
> for all I have not seen.
>
> ·RALPH WALDO EMERSON·

A Treasure Map works best when we focus on one area at a time. Too big a scope is too much for our subconscious to grasp and then nothing much happens. A Treasure Mapping does assist us in the actual lifting of our vision and in seeing images of what we desire in the pictures before us.

You'll need a big piece of posterboard, colored paper, magazines with pictures you can cut up, scissors, glue, markers, pens, glitter, stickers, and real or play money (I personally prefer a real twenty-dollar bill). Also, find a representation of a spiritual symbol that is meaningful to you, a picture of a magnificent sunrise, for instance, or of Jesus or the Buddha or angels.

Now decide what area of your life you want to focus on. Do you want to:

Plan a tour of Europe?

Complete your college degree?

Find and live in love with your soulmate in a holy relationship?

Have a baby?

Advance in your career?

Move into a beautiful new house?

Buy a new car?

Study with a spiritual teacher you admire?

Adopt a happier lifestyle?

After you have chosen your area of focus, close your eyes and "see" what your ideal picture would look like. Be sure to give your picture dimension, color, texture, and form. When you come out of this visualization, gather your materials to decorate your Treasure Map.

Leaf through the magazines for pictures that relate to your focus, and cut them out. With this before you, open your imagination and see yourself already having your desire. Create a visual prayer on your Treasure Map. It is of utmost importance that you also include these essential components:

1. A spiritual symbol. This means God is in the picture.
2. Money (again, real or play). Often we need money to make our dreams a reality.
3. An image of yourself.
4. On the bottom of the Treasure Map, a message such as: "Thank you, Spirit [God], for this or something better." This leaves the door open for something even more fabulous for us than we can currently imagine. You may choose to write an affirmation or two actually on the Map, or clip out and paste on it half a dozen feeling words, such as *blissful, ecstatic, energized, confident, excited, gratified, self-reliant, loving.*

> Imagination is the star in man,
> the celestial or super-celestial body.
>
> ·RULAND THE LEXICOGRAPHER·

When you are finished, place your Treasure Map where you will see it daily. If others in your household do not join you and support your dream one hundred percent, you may choose to have it be for your eyes only. If they think it's silly or won't work, keep it where only you will see it.

I know of a German woman, Rosemarie, who, while living in the United States, needed a new car. She made a Treasure Map, filling it with pictures of German-made cars from magazine advertisements. She cut out the image of the model sitting in the driver's seat in one ad and replaced it with a snapshot of herself smiling broadly and waving out the car window. Rosemarie kept this project to herself. Only a few days passed before she received a phone call from an acquaintance who was moving and wanted to free herself of many possessions, including her quite new, German-made automobile. She told Rosemarie, "I don't know why, but I immediately thought of you, and that you might be interested in the car." She mentioned a fair price. Rosemarie

> The eye with which I see God is the same as that with which he sees me. My eye and the eye of God are one eye, one vision, one knowledge, and one love.
>
> ·MEISTER ECKHART·

went to look at the car—and it was exactly like one of those on her recently made Treasure Map, right down to the same color. She was thrilled that the spiffy little car had found her, and she bought it.

Several years ago I made such a visual prayer, focusing on being published in a wider arena. I desired national magazine articles as my next step, so I devoted my Treasure Map to magazines; of course I included the very important "Thank you, God, for this or something better." To my surprise and joy, God was thinking books! What I received was much more than I had originally been able to grasp.

Why does Treasure Mapping work? Because we are focusing on what we want, and what we focus on does expand. A Treasure Map assists us in conceiving of more good for ourselves. As we work with a Treasure Map, we are mentally conceiving what we desire to achieve.

We must train what Buddhists call our "monkey mind"—that erratic and frantic part of us, conflicted thoughts that are like a pod of wild monkeys frolicking about—before we can begin to perceive truly and behold life through eyes that see through vision, rather than eyes that behold only the illusion. As our seeing is elevated to true vision we do see the light. We understand more and question less. We see ourselves and all others in love rather than fear. We see the beauty of the truth of God shining in all we look upon.

> The heart is nothing but the Sea of Light,
> the place of the vision of God.
>
> ·RUMI·

> If your eye be single, your whole body will be filled with light.
>
> ·JESUS CHRIST·

A few years ago, the son of a friend of mine was trying to decide what college to attend. He had applied to and been accepted by several schools, and had narrowed the list to three or four. All fit his academic requirements, all were about the same size, and all were roughly the same distance from home. He knew he was qualified for them all, but the final selection was difficult. He would have to visit the schools themselves. He made appointments to talk to the admissions officer of each school, and arranged for walking tours of the campuses.

After visiting the first two schools he was even more confused about how to make this important decision. His mother had gone with him, and sensing his confusion, she suggested he try to visualize himself at each school, walking the campus, going to classes, and living in a dorm. Could he see himself happy, content, successful, and peaceful at the school? The feeling didn't come until they visited the last school, Ohio University in Athens. As he walked that campus, and only that campus, he could "see" himself living happily, comfortably, and achieving his goals. Trusting his inner eye worked magnificently. He was indeed happy there, earning two degrees in four years, graduating cum laude, and making friends to last a lifetime. He is now a marketing coordinator for an entertainment company in California, and the memories of his college years are precious to him.

See yourself with the same sight as God sees you. Remember Meister Eckhart's words, "My eye and the eye of God are one eye, one vision, one knowledge and one love." See yourself in this light and your dreams will swiftly become your reality.

Learning to Lighten Up

The Spiritual Law of Joy

5

The state of joy can be constant. It does, however, take an unwavering commitment. When our minds are filled with dark and fearful thoughts, we can't imagine that this would be possible.

Joy is so like love that it is nearly impossible to distinguish one from the other. It is not possible to be in a state of total love without realizing joy as well. When our minds are no longer split, we will quite naturally know joy.

Now or in the past we have all sought joy and happiness within hollow and even harmful experiences, from remaining in dysfunctional relationships, to seeking solitude in alcohol or in drugs, to pursuing any kind of addictive behavior. Many people tolerate tremendous pain while futilely searching for joy in such behaviors, until dawn breaks within their consciousness and they realize there must be a better way.

A *Course in Miracles* teaches, "Those who let illusions be lifted from their minds are the world's saviors." When we let the

> The soul is here for its own joy.
>
> ·RUMI·

illusion of finding pleasure through pain go from our minds, we also let separation and duality go from our minds. We then experience oneness, in the beginning for just a moment. For a brief instant we do not see our interests as apart from those of others. For a holy instant we see no distinction between what had previously been perceived as separate. Separation is a state where our minds are split. Separation is the decision to not know ourselves. Even though a deep inner part of us may be in tune with the divine, the rest is in intense conflict.

Have you ever had a moment of oneness? If you have, take some time and write about it. Describe it in full detail, and if it has happened more than once, write about the first time, the most profound time, the most recent time. Have these moments of oneness had any lasting effects on your life? Have they had any lasting effects on your knowing?

An older gentleman friend of mine, Tom, related to me how as a young man he was led into a deep state of meditation. While centered in this state he "saw" the interior of an unfamiliar restaurant. When his attention and focus returned to his normal outer awareness he could still "see" this restaurant in his mind's eye. He sketched the scene flashing through his consciousness and wrote a description of what it felt and smelled like.

Several days later a business associate called and set up a lunchtime meeting near his office. As Tom rode the bus across town, the restaurant interior kept flashing into his awareness. He shook his head in an attempt to rid himself of the recurring image, then chose to walk the last couple of blocks. While walking he began wondering exactly why this business acquaintance had called him. Still lost in thought, Tom entered the restaurant. The next instant he nearly lost his breath and his balance.

Tom found himself standing in the midst of his recurring image. There before him, in living color and great detail, was the outer picture of this haunting inner image. A shaken Tom proceeded to the table where his acquaintance was sitting. Tom was doing his best to compose himself and process what was happening, when the business associate surprised him even more. Tom's associate offered him a magnificent position, one that immediately doubled his salary.

Why had Tom received that image of the restaurant? He believed, and I concur, that it was his inner Spirit knocking at the door of his consciousness, saying, "Tom, you are ready for more. There is so much more to life than you have ever imagined, and here is a glimpse of what is possible." Not only did Tom accept the position that was offered, but from that moment on he committed his life, including his new career, to a new, exciting, and richly rewarding way of living in the moment; he understood from his own personal experience that he was not alone. He knew he had a part to play in a reality much larger than he had dreamed possible.

As we begin to awaken to our true selves, and commune more and more with our inner being, it dawns on us how very blessed we are as sons and daughters of God. So often we see ourselves as restricted and limited in countless ways. We view our health, or lack of it, and other traits as the result of genes inherited from a family member. We have our father's poor eyesight, our mother's quick temper, our grandfather's baldness, or money slips through our fingers just like Uncle Seymour's.

The spiritual truth of your being is that we don't have

anyone's poor eyesight but our own. Our poor eyesight is only ours, as is our quick temper or poor financial position. The good news is that they are ours only as long as we claim them. If we claim ourselves instead as blessed sons or daughters of God, we will experience blessings.

Here is a wonderful exercise: Three times an hour, affirm to yourself: "I am blessed as a beloved son/daughter of God." Now, your day may include experiences that speak more of conflict than of blessing. If this is so, it is especially important to remind yourself: "I am blessed as a beloved son/daughter of God." At the close of each day consider some of the joyous things to which you are entitled as a blessed son or daughter of God. Write a list out and add to it each night. Here is a sample:

> I am blessed as a son/daughter of God.
>
> I deserve to work in a supportive environment.
>
> I deserve to have a healed relationship with my partner.
>
> I deserve fun and joy in my life.
>
> I deserve an easier financial flow.
>
> I am blessed as a beloved son/daughter of God.
>
> I deserve to feel great physically.
>
> I am blessed as a son/daughter of God, and I am in my blessed state learning to lighten up.
>
> I am blessed as a son/daughter of God, and I am learning to let go of the struggle.

Make your own list nightly and examine how blessed you are. Whenever you feel "off" in any way, affirm again this truth of your being, and you will experience the larger reality of hov blessed you are as God's beloved son or daughter.

Working with the idea that we are blessed as God's children helps us accept in the present that which is true in the eternal. Within you now is everything that is perfect, waiting to radiate through you into the world. You can never be deprived of your blessedness, but you can deprive yourself of knowing it. That is why it is beneficial to affirm frequently, "I am blessed as a son/daughter of God." The affirmation helps us remember what is eternally true.

When we feel anything but blessed, we are letting fear and separation enter our lives. This is always a sure sign that we are moving through life relying solely on our own strength. And when we do so, we have reason to be fearful. When we rely on our strength alone, we are relying on ego. We are in a state of denial of our divine heritage as sons and daughters of God, and allow our egos to rule rather than our spirit. We experience fearful consequences that are a result of fear-filled states of mind.

Before moving into a new experience or going to an important meeting or interview, I always affirm this blessing: "The spirit of God goes before me, making my way smooth, easy, joyous, successful, and clear." It always works for me. The way is open, the encounter goes easily and smoothly. There is a joy-filled connection, and I feel success for all involved.

When we are in denial of our divine power and our spiritual heritage, our fear-filled minds are affirming: "All the fears of my ego mind go before me, making my way twisted, bumpy, difficult, glum, unsuccessful, and dark." And what do we receive as a result of such negative affirming? Miserable encounters. Obviously such negative affirmations lead to negative results, and yet so many times I hear people arguing for their limitations.

> Beauty saves. Beauty heals. Beauty motivates. Beauty unites. Beauty returns us to our origins, and here lies the ultimate act of saving, of healing, of overcoming dualism. Beauty allows us to forget the pain and dwell on the joy.
>
> ·MATTHEW FOX·

Richard Bach reminds us of this in *Illusions:* "Argue for your limitations and sure enough they're yours."

When we argue that no one can be trusted, what we are really saying is that we don't trust ourselves. When we argue that there are no opportunities, the message actually is that we're afraid to step out and seek our dreams. When we argue that life is always a struggle, the reality is that we don't know what we'd be without the struggle, because it has become our identity. We empower our reasons and excuses, rather than ourselves. We give power to certain upset and disappointment, rather than accept our blessings and live our joy.

A spiritual truth is: We can always trust another when we have worked through our own trust issues. When we live in integrity, our word is our honor; we bless others and ourselves with it, and we know it's safe for us to trust ourselves. Therefore we can trust others. After working through our own trust issues, we attract only trustworthy individuals. Another spiritual truth: There are unlimited opportunities in this world for us, and our lives are meant to be happy. If we don't believe this now, it is because this truth is buried deep within, under many veils and walls of separation, fearful and even insane thoughts. We have been relying on our own strength, denying the power of the relationship with our Source. We have every reason to be fearful, anxious, and apprehensive.

As we more fully embrace our oneness with God, it is only natural that we lighten up. We can easily tap into the wellspring of joy bubbling up from our depths.

Cause and Effect

According to a basic law of physics, for every action there is an equal and opposite reaction. This law of cause and effect is at work in the physical world, and also forever at work within us. When God and our divine inheritance are the cause, then the effects (the outer picture of our lives) are a life that is happy, a life that works, a life that has vision, purpose, direction, joy, and loveliness. Cause always precedes effect—there are no exceptions. Life begins within and then is projected outward into the picture of our lives.

We must learn to lighten up, and in order to lighten up we must realize that the Light is within, not hidden somewhere. Many have written about the Light. There are those who have experienced it, there are those who have become one with it. To me, the Light is the purity of God expressed through us individually. When we have removed the major barriers of dark and heavy clouds of fear and separation and erroneous thought, the brilliant inner Light is revealed to us.

Meditation on Finding the Inner Light

A meditation in the workbook of *A Course in Miracles* was my inspiration in creating a meditation practice supportive in

> The strength and the happiness of a man consist in finding out the way in which God is going, and going in that way, too.
>
> ·HENRY WARD BEECHER·

moving toward the Light. You may practice this meditation as often as you desire. I suggest you do it several times a week until you reach the inner Light, and do it to quickly remove any dark clouds that intrude on your peace of mind.

Find a place where you can be undisturbed and quiet for twenty minutes, and sit in a comfortable position. Close your eyes gently, breathe in and out deeply, and let go of the thoughts that generally fill your mind. Think of your mind as a vast circle, surrounded by a layer of heavy, dark clouds. You can see only the clouds, because you are standing outside the circle and quite apart from it. From where you stand, you can see no reason to believe there is a brilliant light behind those clouds. The clouds are all there is to see.

Consider these clouds a metaphor for judgment of guilt and grievances and idle wishes in your life. Do not become entangled in the details; simply be the observer of all this. Now consider what a valuable and important undertaking this healing meditation is, and the enormous worth in what you are doing. Take several slow, deep breaths and move into a state of quiet stillness. Remain focused and determined to move past the clouds of grievances that have darkened your holiness, to reach the light within you.

Imagine yourself now extending your arms and touching the clouds in your mind, and easily brushing them aside with your hands. Experience the sensation of clouds resting on your cheeks, brow, and eyelids, and your gently brushing them aside and going through them. You can do this easily; clouds cannot stop you. Continue to move through the clouds. You are free. You are powerful. Nothing can prevail against you. The only things that have disturbed your peace of mind, held you in darkness, are mere clouds, and clouds cannot stop you.

As you continue with this meditation, you will sense a deep release and feel that you are being lifted and carried ahead. Hold the thought that God is with you, fully supporting your effort and magnifying it a hundredfold. The power of the entire universe is supporting your effort and determination in moving through the dark clouds of your life and into the inner light, the Light of God. You must succeed in this endeavor. The Light will be revealed to you. Your small determination and holy purpose, undertaken with God, must succeed. The Light will come, will dawn within your holy mind. When your mind is filled with only light, you will know only the Light. When this occurs, you will feel complete with the meditation. Now you may take several deep breaths in and out, to feel a deep sense of release, and peace.

This exercise clears the consciousness of the density blocking the connection with the Divine. People have reported to me that they could feel the clouds and sense themselves pushing them away. I have been told of flashing brilliant golden-white light, as well as simply of a gradual lifting of the gray clouds and the dawning of the Light. Your experience will be unique to you, and yet universal. The Light is there, and the only thing blocking it from your awareness is some flimsy, dense-looking clouds—really nothing at all.

Once we have glimpsed the inner Light, we can never again deny our inner resources and who we are as divine sons and

> As we are now living in an eternity, the time to be happy is today.
>
> ·GRENVILLE KLEISER·

daughters. As we join with the inner Light, it not only radiates through our individual expression of life but also "spreads across the world in quiet joy," as *A Course in Miracles* describes. Touching the inner Light reminds us to lighten up in other areas of our lives:

To lighten up in our attitude.

To lighten up a serious nature.

To lighten up in our ability to overlook minor inconveniences and troubles.

To lighten up in our judgments of ourselves and others.

To lighten up and have more fun.

A Teaspoon of Sand

One of my favorite pleasures is a romantic picnic lunch with my husband on a secluded beach. David, not being overly fond of sand, would prefer to eat at home on our porch or at a restaurant. One day he agreed to go with me to the beach for a picnic. I wanted to make this experience extraordinary, so David would really enjoy it. I knew he would see that even though he's not crazy about sand, he could have a great day at the beach.

I didn't make just an ordinary picnic lunch, I created a feast, with salade Niçoise and other yummy things to eat. We loaded the car with straw mats, a pile of giant towels, beach chairs (to keep David out of the sand as much as possible), beach toys, an inflatable raft, binoculars—everything imaginable, because I wanted David to appreciate the beach and see how wonderful lunch on a secluded stretch could be.

We arrived at the shore, and not another soul was in sight. The setting was gorgeous beyond description: The ocean was aqua and royal blue, with sparkling highlights reflecting the sun. The sand was white, and there were gently swaying palm trees for shade. While we unloaded the car, an enchanting breeze rustled through the palms. As we laid down the mats and towels, the wind began to pick up slightly. We ran up and down the beach gathering coconuts and placed them around our romantic feast. But the coconuts were not heavy enough to hold everything down against the increasing wind, so we placed our shoes and chairs strategically.

I served our plates as the wind blew with increasing force. We were now sitting with our backs to the wind, hunched over our plates, trying to take it all with a good spirit and enjoy our lunch. It's a challenge to enjoy salade Niçoise with a teaspoon of sand in your mouth. I was beginning to feel very disappointed, and betrayed by the wind ruining our romantic picnic. No sooner had I thought that than the wind picked up one of the plastic chairs (despite the coconut meant to weigh it down) and brought it flying into my head and shoulders. It didn't really hurt me, but it certainly startled me. My romantic fun-o-meter was definitely going down! David and I hunched and huddled closer together and gobbled our gritty lunch. The wind blew even stronger; the sand stung our skin. Finally David risked death by sand inhalation, opening his mouth and softly saying, "Do you think we could leave now? I've had just about all the fun I can stand for one day."

I don't know whether it was what he said or that he said it so gently because he knew how much I valued a day at the beach, but I started to laugh hysterically. This got David laughing just as hard. We had to cover our faces to shield them from the beating sand as we laughed so hard we cried. Without a word we jumped up and raced to dismantle what remained of our romantic picnic, and threw it in the car. We drove home still laughing about our adventure at the beach.

Later that day, reflecting on what happened, I was thankful to live in the consciousness of seeing the lighter side of life, thankful we didn't blame each other or make ourselves miserable with what others might have thought of as a ruined afternoon. We could see the humor in this fiasco.

A fun, and perhaps rather silly, technique can help us learn to lighten up. I've known it to work best in a group setting, but it can help just as well with one person. Say aloud—simultaneously if you are with others—"Ha, ha, ha, ha." You can say this with mirth and delight, silliness, or seriousness. The key is to keep doing it—don't stop. After several minutes you won't be saying, "Ha, ha, ha, ha," you'll be doubled over in glee. You'll be in the wonderful release of an endorphin rush.

G. K. Chesterton said, "Angels can fly because they take themselves lightly." When we learn to look within and find the Light, we can take ourselves and all of life lightly and allow our spirits to fly too. When we are aware of living in the Light, we can give all of life the Light touch. We can remember to turn our difficult times and challenges over to the Light, to lighten up in all circumstances, to seek the joyous rather than cling to old grievances.

One of the most effective ways I know for this lightening-up process is to learn not to take personally someone else's "stuff." This takes work, diligence, as well as an unwavering inner commitment to live in peace and joy rather than struggle and conflict.

Here's an easy consciousness test to ascertain whether something is your stuff or someone else's. If you can remain the dispassionate observer of another person's behavior, it's not your stuff. If you react with outrage, disgust, fear, or judgment, then whatever is occurring is presenting you with a valuable lesson. Simply stated: Reaction—it's your stuff. No reaction—it's not your stuff. Any reaction is a sure sign that you have further healing work to do in that area. When a colleague, friend, or family member is behaving poorly, you must learn not to engage in that drama. Rather than meet drama with drama, upset with upset, you can send that individual love and compassion, knowing that the person must be in pain and suffering or he or she would not be behaving so poorly.

Over the past several years I have found a very helpful Buddhist teaching that is relevant here. Buddhists speak of people exhibiting "unskilled behavior." This is acknowledged without judgment or condemnation; it is simply observed with compassion. In a particular moment, if a person could have behaved differently, he or she would have. Instead of cursing or judging, Buddhists bless with compassion, knowing the person must be in pain to inflict pain through words or actions.

When we can see without judgment, our souls are free to know joy. We can behold another person not as "jerk" or "wicked" or "bad," but rather as someone who is in that moment exhibiting unskilled behavior. When making such an observation myself, I add this question: "Haven't I too exhibited unskilled behavior under similar circumstances?" When we are honest with ourselves, the answer will always be yes. We may not have acted out the behavior, but certainly we have thought about doing so.

Once we have learned to lighten up and live in a joyous, happy state, our power to manifest the desires of our hearts is *greatly* magnified. We will find our good rushing forward to greet us from every direction. Life becomes a constant celebration.

Laura Bell Jones, in her book *Jesus CEO*, tells of encountering a young man who tells her he has chilled champagne in the trunk of his car and invites her to join him in a toast. She's surprised that someone would have champagne chilling in his trunk and asks, "Do you always carry champagne in your trunk?" "Oh, yes!" he replies. "Life is full of opportunities to celebrate, and I don't want to miss any of them."

How often do you stop and celebrate life? Think of a recent event that could have been celebrated and that instead you let slip by. How could you have done things differently? Are you willing to do things differently? Are you willing to do things differently the next time? Will you remember? Like the young man with the champagne, will you be prepared? He was *always* expecting something worthy of a celebration to occur, and surely he is constantly drawing remarkable events to himself.

The outer world can so quickly cloud the inner Light that we lose touch with our center of joy. We forget to celebrate, and we lose our ability to wonder. We can become so caught up in the everyday affairs of life, the little and the mundane, that we forget to stop and celebrate, to enjoy and live in the exquisite wonder of it all.

God created the laws of joy for you so that you could live here and now in a happy state. When we are at one with the inner Light and living in a state of joy, we create beauty in our lives as a natural expression of who and what we are. We will no longer be able to contain our joy. The dark and little world of our past will vanish like the clouds from our meditation that return to the nothingness out of which they first rose. Can you imagine what life would be like with your heart filled with joy?

The ego thinks that to live in such a state must be very difficult. Living thus need not be difficult, but it will be different. It is joy that we all really want. As we join with the Light of God within, we take our rightful place as the beloved sons or daughters of God who have at long last awakened from a long sleep. We move into the Light and take our rightful place as Divine heirs.

Getting Out of "Poor Me"

The Spiritual Law of Power 6

The limitless creative power of God is available to each of us. But we must be available to this creative power. We all have enormous power; we have just lost our awareness of it. So it appears unavailable to us, and we appear helpless and weak to ourselves. We see ourselves as victims, not much-loved children of God. When we are living in our self-created world of victimhood, the great truth of our spiritual power is obscure, or even nonexistent, to us.

In this chapter we will explore how we give our power away and deny ourselves our true worth. We will examine how we imprison ourselves and how, on the other hand, we can transform our pain-filled lives. We must be willing to release the false concepts we have clung to and learn to embrace who and what we are, God's precious sons and daughters. We can let the past and its pain go, but only if we are willing to have a new, free, empowered life.

We must be willing to embrace our magnificence and no longer accept our littleness. We have the choice not to see ourselves as helpless or imposed upon or unappreciated. It is within our command to perceive ourselves as lovable, capable, appreciated, and powerful. There is nothing the power of God within us cannot do.

Power transforms energy from one plane to another; it moves mountains of negativity, doubt, and resistance. The energy of spirit causes vibrations that open a way where previously there seemed to be none. This awakened power is not about controlling or changing other people; this would be misuse of it. It *is* about taking control over our own experiences, our own lives, and changing or, more specifically, transforming ourselves.

There is an enormous difference between change, a minor adjustment or alteration, and transformation, a complete metamorphosis. Change is a chameleon going from tan to green, transformation is a caterpillar emerging as a glorious butterfly.

Picture yourself as a generator filled with crackling energy that you have kept carefully concealed, under heavy guard. On an inner level you always know this great force is available at any moment; all it takes is your command to unleash this force. Consider this when you are tempted to view yourself as a victim, as small and inconsequential. You are in actuality attempting to reconcile the unreconcilable—combining attack (which you feel is being done to you) with innocence (which you inwardly know to be the truth of your being)—to the extent that you believe you have nothing to do with what shows up in your life. You do what many of us do, try to convince ourselves that we are simply innocent victims.

Our healing begins when we say yes to our own power and no longer agree to be helpless victims. We no longer seek to

> The non-violent approach does not immediately change the heart of the oppressor. It first does something to the hearts and souls of those committed to it. It gives them a new self-respect; it calls up resources of strength and courage that they did not know they had. Finally it reaches the opponent and so stirs his conscience that reconciliation becomes a reality.
>
> ·MARTIN LUTHER KING, JR.·

combine what can never unite: attack and innocence. When we accept the power of God as ours and are willing to use it wisely, it indicates that we have connected with the Light and remember who and what we are. It is through the correct use of power that we master ourselves, not another person. Power is not to be exercised on other people, but on ourselves.

Many do not embrace the power locked within their spiritual nature because they do not understand it and are fearful of it. We are unable to overcome our fears until we attain some realization of spiritual power, dominion, and mastery over the circumstances of our lives. We cannot break through the barriers of littleness and limitation without engaging the potential locked within us. When we are in victim consciousness, a weakened or wounded state of mind, we lose our power. Yet this loss is temporary; our power is not gone forever.

I have observed that often the way we lose our power is by giving it away. Years ago, I gave my power away to my former husbands. Their accepting my "gift" infuriated me. I felt victimized and powerless. When I went to my first counseling session, as a young woman of twenty-three, I was miserable, crying every day. When I related the pitiful details of my life to the counselor, she said, "You sound like a doormat." I was sobbing but managed to croak out, "Yes, yes, you're right. I am a doormat." She calmly responded, "In order to be a doormat, you have to lie down first." The Light broke through! I had relinquished my power, my own mastery, by lying down and *allowing* someone to walk over me. That realization was one of the most transforming of my life.

Did I immediately stand up, reclaim my power, and walk away? No, but the realization had been made, and a deep inner shift began. After that session, whenever I gave my power away, I recognized it. It's not that I never did it again, because I did, but at least I knew *I* was doing it, it wasn't someone doing it to me.

Consider how you have handed over your power, and to whom. Perhaps it is your spouse, current or former. Perhaps it is your mother, father, child, co-worker, or boss, or a corporation, the government, or educators.

We give our power away when we allow ourselves to become upset over another person's behavior. We give our power away when we refuse to forgive and release a hurt from the past. Our power, given away, keeps that old wound festering in the present. We give our power away when we believe we cannot live without another person. Indeed, we can even imprison ourselves when we give our power away.

God has given us the power to create. We must remember that we always have a choice. We have free will. We can decide whether to use our power constructively or destructively. We can choose to give it away or to empower ourselves. The power of the divine fills each of us, and all we need do is claim it. Claiming it means giving up being the doormat, no longer leading with our

> For in truth, in this world, hatred is not appeased by hatred. Hatred is appeased by love alone. This is the eternal law.
>
> ·DHAMMAPADA·

wounds. We become joyous and confident people who take responsibility for our lives. We must remember: Only I can imprison myself, only I can set myself free.

Nothing can hurt me unless I give it the power to do so.

Nothing can make me mad, bad, sad, or glad.

Memorize these empowering affirmations, and repeat them whenever you are tempted to give your power away. Nothing can hurt you, or change you in any way, except yourself. When you have reclaimed your power, you realize this to be so.

Release and Replace

If there is something unpleasant in your life, a sure way to keep it and have it loom even larger is to talk about how awful it is to everyone you encounter, or to rehash it to yourself, rerunning it in your mind like an endless-loop tape. This is how you give power to something negative.

To transform a negative situation and diminish its negative effects, cease thinking about it and talking about it to everyone you meet. Whenever a disturbing circumstance comes into your mind, release it to the Light; replace the old thought with a new spiritual thought—a divine thought or any loving, true, transforming idea. Look at the situation differently; when you do this, you will be using your power constructively.

A key to happiness and success is to give your power to what you want, never to what you don't want. An easy way to remember this: *What I focus on expands.*

Focus on pain—pain expands.

Focus on lack—lack expands.

Focus on anger—anger expands.

Focus on another's negative attitude—
the negative attitude expands.

Focus on healing—healing expands.

Focus on love—love expands.

Focus on peace—peace expands.

Focus on goodness—goodness expands.

Focus on what you have, positive or negative—
what you have expands.

It's very simple. Don't try to make it complicated. Complication is of the ego. Simplicity is of the Spirit. Do an experiment now: Consider what you have been focusing your conversations on, consider your thoughts and the feelings attached to these thoughts.

Now consider what has been present in your life. There is a direct link between what you focus on and what is present in your outer world. *A Course in Miracles* reminds us of this Spiritual Reality: "Your inner and outer worlds are actually the same." Until our minds are clear, we see them as different. Trust that they are not. We create all manner of misery for ourselves when

> For as long as space exists and sentient beings endure,
> May I too remain, to dispel the misery of the world.
>
> ·SHANTIDEVA·

we hold to the belief that we are powerless and had nothing to do with its creation. When we are in denial of our power, we perceive that what we have in our lives is just there. It simply happens, and then we think about it, talk about it, over and over. When we empower ourselves, we recognize that *we* are keeping alive the various situations in life by constantly focusing on them. Not only are we keeping them alive, but we are actually creating them.

Ask yourself: Do I desire a world that I am in charge of, or one that is in charge of me? Do I desire a world where I am powerful or powerless? What is your answer? Not your instant outer answer, but the answer of your subconscious mind and soul. On this deep level of mind can you declare with certainty that you want to claim your power? Of course!

Years ago, I thought I was a victim. But when I realized I didn't have to be a victim, I put aside my victim mentality. You can do the same, you can do something about it. You, like me, can get up off the floor, and draw your misplaced power back to yourself. The most empowering work I did for this was the deep breath work called rebirthing. The concept of breath work has broadened immensely in recent years and has taken a number of different slants. If the idea resonates with you, explore what is available in your area, or travel to attend a workshop with some of the leaders in breath work today, such as Stanislas and Christina Grof, or facilitators trained in Loving Relationships Training (LRT).

When we store up unprocessed anger or unresolved conflict of any kind, we use the tremendous force of our power not to create wonder in our lives, but rather to hold our anger and conflict at bay, to control them in order to function in life. When this occurs, we feel weak, lifeless; we may even be prone to physical problems. We are living in the crater of a volcano that may erupt at any moment. This is very harmful to us physically and extremely disturbing to our peace of mind. While living in this manner, we constantly deny our magnificence. We are imprisoned, our true reality longing to be released.

The great truth of our being is that we are Spiritual Beings living in a Spiritual Universe governed by Spiritual Law. But if we deny our true reality, we give lip service to these words and continue to live as if they were the furthest thing from the truth. We live as if we were isolated. We live as if we were victims. We live as if we were powerless, controlled by circumstances, forgetting who we are, forgetting all that has been graciously given to us. We must practice and practice until living out of our released spiritual power is second nature to us. Only then can we take our rightful place as co-creators with God. I love the line from *A Course in Miracles:* "God has given you a place in His Mind forever."

For a moment consider this: The thought of you is held in the Mind of God, not just for an instant, but forever. Not a bad place to be. God offers everything to us, all peace, all love, all fulfillment, all joy. "No, thank you," we say. "I want to play in the dark a bit longer and pretend that I'm lost and alone and that there are monsters out there that terrify me and will eat me alive if I'm not shrewd enough." God says, "Oh, okay, but are you sure you'd rather not come into the Light and experience a bit of bliss?" "No," we respond, "bliss is for others! I'd rather struggle. Thanks anyway." We would rather scare ourselves with the monsters in the dark. It gives us an adrenaline rush, and then we know we're alive.

In my past, I realize, I created some horrific situations, got the adrenaline rush, cried out in frantic desperation for help, and invited God to the rescue. I had to be reminded once again that it needn't be this difficult, that everything is going to be all right. It's as if God would always ask, "Have you suffered enough? Are you sufficiently traumatized and ready to try another way?"

A key component of our becoming personally empowered is to face our greatest fears and overcome them. Until we do so the fears will continue to control us. When we have many fears, our vital personal energy does not empower us, it tries to conceal those fears. "Feel your fear and do it anyway" means that you tap into your own power and release it, with fear as the fuel to boost you, not consume you.

There are contrived ways of "feeling your fear and doing it anyway," such as firewalking, bungee jumping, rappelling down a mountain, and on and on. There are also life opportunities that allow us to face our fears and rise triumphant on the other side: dealing with a life-threatening illness, for instance, or handling the loss of a loved one through death or divorce, or coping with any profound life-altering occurrence. Our fears may be more specific, such as fear of spiders, snakes, or mice. We may fear being alone, or fear crowds, water, or old age. Fear is never valuable, and it is always a way to chip away at your power. We all have some fear lurking in the dark recesses of our subconscious, but in any distressing situation we can learn to face the fear and engage the power of God within us to overcome it. Our fears have imprisoned us only because we have believed it was possible to imprison God's holy son or daughter. What we need to do is recognize that the doors to our personal prison have never been locked. We have been forever free, and need merely to swing the door open and walk out into freedom. This is the right use of our power.

While staying for a month in a vacation rental, I had to face one of my lingering fears—*mice.* There are people who would rather face an IRS audit, or a tooth extraction without anesthesia, than stand up before an assembled body of contemporaries and give a speech. Well, I stand up before people weekly to teach and speak, and I am a hundred percent at ease. I could stand before a million people and be completely comfortable and natural, but let a teeny mouse run by me and I shriek! In one week I saw three mice on two different occasions. My husband saw zero. Of course he's not terrified of mice and could not understand my hysteria at all. Meanwhile I kept seeing mice. Once I opened the silverware drawer to find a furry gray critter staring up at me. My knees immediately turned to Jell-O!

Neither of us is into killing anything, so it was a dilemma what to do. David wanted to let the mice be and let them use the house as their play yard. I spent a day searching for humane traps until finally locating two; we caught a few mice and released them into the woods. David flew home while I stayed on to finish a writing project. I hoped the mouse scare was over. Wrong!

I walked into the living room one day to find a dead one. I screamed despite the fact there was nobody around to hear me. I realized there also was no one around to take care of the corpse but me. I considered putting a bucket over it and never entering the room again. It did occur to me that perhaps that was an immature solution, and that the smell would become intolerable. What to do? I got a trashcan and put it right next to the corpse, making a point not to look at the remains. Then I put a paper towel over the mouse, again intent on not looking at it, and

> Follow your bliss.
>
> ·JOSEPH CAMPBELL·

scooped it up with a dustpan and brush. It moved slightly and I screamed, but by God, I did it. It wasn't a happy or pleasant thing to do, and I don't want to do it again anytime soon, but I did it. It's a silly fear, but I faced it and handled it on my own. When we feel the fear and do it anyway, the fear no longer has a life-denying grip on us.

Power is mastery over your life:

The energy of the divine in expression.

The assertion of your authority as a blessed being.

The full declaration of the truth of your being.

The claim to your sacred heritage.

The recognition of the significance of your spoken words.

The ability to transform energy from one plane to another.

Your personal declaration of independence.

Claiming your power is freedom!

An Exercise in Claiming Your Power

Until we are clear and secure in our personal power, it is helpful to remind ourselves in the face of any threat or upset that we are not the victims in a particular situation or of a particular person.

As we affirm this, we declare our release from the imprisoning chains that we have forged for ourselves. For most of us the tightest chains on us are those we perceive in our own minds. In order to loosen these links in the chain, you may need to repeat this exercise a number of times throughout the day. When you feel the slightest temptation to think yourself unfairly treated or victimized, declare with passion and power: "I am not the victim here! I claim my power! I claim my power now! This situation [or person] has no power over me!"

Apply these ideas diligently to your inner world as well as your outer world. They are a declaration of your freedom and a refusal to live any longer in bondage. It is unacceptable and it will not continue. The empowered have what they want in life. Victims only create more and more misery.

An Exercise to Tap into Spiritual Power

We move through six stages as we tap into our Divine Power. Our experience of personal power begins in the inner recesses of our being in the *silence.* It progresses to the conscious level as a *thought:* "This need not be. I am not powerless here. I am not the victim of this situation." It moves on to the outer declaration of the thought, the *spoken word*, which brings *release* to the old, blocked energy. Then comes a *clearing*, from whose emptiness a different outcome, a new *outer manifestation*, can be born.

Stage 1. Silence

Stage 2. Thought

Stage 3. Spoken Word

> It's not the earthquake that controls
> the advent of a different life.
> But storms of generosity and visions
> of incandescent souls.
>
> ·BORIS PASTERNAK·

Stage 4. Release

Stage 5. Clearing

Stage 6. Outer Manifestation

Tap into your own Divine Power with the six stages in mind. First, enter a meditative state and be in the silence. Light is pure, raw power awaiting your direction. Second, allow a spiritualized thought to enter your mind and begin its particular vibration. Third, speak a word that is either audible or inaudible. Fourth, release all inner feelings of fear and doubt. Fifth, clear everything away to enter the empty state of pure potential. Sixth, experience the new outcome of the previous states.

My friend Ginna Bragg, a talented gourmet chef and a coauthor of *A Simple Celebration,* entered into a complex legal partnership for a celebrated food operation. She was the only woman among several high-powered and demanding professional men. Ginna lives her life with a great commitment to harmony and balance. She knows her product and what she brings to the negotiating table very well. She does not, however, have much experience dealing with money moguls who have a "new plan" every other week.

These powerful men communicated individually to Ginna what they wanted her to do. This frustrated and confused her, and it didn't seem much of a partnership. When one of the men said to her, "We'll get back to you on Monday and let you know what we want you to do," she did not sit back and play the victim. She went within and sought her own counsel. She "got back" to that man—and to each of the others—sending a fax that told them: This is who I am, this is what I do, and this is what I have to offer. Period.

Ginna had a choice. She could have felt like the victim of these forceful and opinionated men and given them her power, or she could empower herself and remind them of who she was and what she had to bring to the table. She did not sit by and wring her hands together waiting for them to "get back" to her. How did she feel, taking so much power into her hands? She felt fabulous and in charge of her life. How did the men respond? The spokesman for the group immediately called her and exclaimed how enlightened she was. When we take back our power and empower ourselves, doors that have been closed open. Minds that have been closed open.

When we have been locked as victims within the walls of our limited consciousness, we view the world as a painful place of constant struggle, where God's sons and daughters are forever imprisoned. As we awaken from our long sleep of dark and disturbing states of mind, the truth dawns on us that the world is our prison only if and when we enter the cell. The world is where we can be free.

With this realization, the light of the eternal truth of our holiness shines through the darkness, showing us that the way to freedom lies deep within ourselves. Our inner holiness is unlimited in its ability to restore our lives to limitless joy, happiness, wonder, and power.

Principles of Love

The Spiritual Law of Love 7

While I was on tour with *A Course in Love*, I was most frequently asked the question "How do you define love?" I remember one man in a large crowd asking, "Would you define love as an emotion or a decision?" I thought for a moment, unable to restrict myself to the two choices he offered, and then answered, "Neither. I see love as a spiritual power, the eternal essence of who and what we are. Love is the glue of the Universe that holds all of life together. It is the great cosmic adhesive."

Spiritual love is unconditional. It does not demand or fight for its own way. Love knows and sees only completion. Love is always freeing; it never binds us or attempts to control us. Love has the power to bring all things, all minds, all conditions into their right and highest relationship with everything. Love is the idea of Universal unity. It is the living of our oneness. Love, true love, is another name for God.

So often, when our thinking is aligned with the world and its

> A loving heart is the truest wisdom.
>
> ·CHARLES DICKENS·

limited ways of relating, we perceive love as something we get from another person rather than what it truly is: the formative energy of our being. Love is not a commodity, it is our essence. There are not different kinds of love called for in different circumstances. Love cannot be divided, factored, or portioned out. Love is Infinite, Divine. Love is One. It comes from God and is our true nature and Divine heritage. While we dwell in painful states, we erect many barriers to love, defenses against it, and convoluted appeals for it.

All such activity comes from our ego, mightily at work to hold love's presence just beyond the grasp of our awareness. The ego rules by fear. The Spirit guides through love. Love is not a concept we study to learn more about. It is the soul quality that we all possess. We remember love as something we have always known. What we must learn is that love is not bartering, conditional giving, withholding, sacrifice, conflict-filled division, entanglement with fear, or something forever changing. Love does not limit, or divide, or express itself one way for one person and another way for another. Love is one. Love offers everything to everyone eternally. It is forever changeless and without alteration. Love enters your mind and enters gladly at your invitation.

We must recognize, examine, and release the countless barriers to love's presence that have ruled our minds. These barriers have not brought us peace and joy. They have kept us living in pain and separation.

In this chapter we shall learn to release ourselves from these barriers and to remember the love of God that has always been with us, awaiting our invitation to come forth and set life right by making its ways known to us once again. I learned from *A Course in Miracles* years ago that "when you want only love, you will see nothing else." Love is of God. You are of God and were created in love to extend God's love to all.

Love Versus Fear

Spiritually, we may look at life as one of two possible expressions: love or a cry for love. Think of any condition or circumstance, from a holy relationship, which is love, to a dysfunctional relationship, which is a cry for love. Kind, compassionate behavior is love in expression, while unskilled behavior (temper tantrums, pouting, gossiping, sulking) is a cry for love. One extends from the Spirit, which is love itself; the other comes from the ego, which is ruled by fear. It is liberating to observe our own behavior as either love or a cry for love, an expression of the love or of the fear within us.

Here's a helpful exercise. You'll need paper and pen and a quiet place where you won't be disturbed. Think of a recent situation in which you were upset. Write a brief description of what occurred and what you felt. Next, make two columns, headed "A Call for Love" and "Love," and break down the described situation in those two columns. See the example below.

A woman named Kathy wrote:

While Bill and I were out at a party Saturday night, his old girlfriend showed up, and he left me to go outside and talk to her. They talked for twenty minutes, while I sat alone and felt terribly uncomfortable. When he returned, I said nothing and soon after asked to go home. I think he still really cares for his former girlfriend, and I'm just in his life to fill a void. He's called several times and left messages saying he was sorry about his talking to his old flame, but it was necessary, and he would like to talk to me to clear up any misunderstanding.

Here's how Kathy completed the two columns:

A Call for Love	Love
Bill left me at the party.	Bill has called several times.
I felt alone and uncomfortable.	He wants to clear up the misunderstanding.
I said nothing.	I still have deep feelings for Bill.
I asked to go home.	
He cares for his old girlfriend.	
I'm a void filler.	

Kathy needed to examine soulfully what occurred and see how her own fears and insecurities were rising to the surface in this relationship. Since she was willing to talk with Bill, she learned that his ex-girlfriend had been giving him some unsettling news about her health, and he was simply being supportive. Kathy's insecurities, like ours, were a call for love.

When we are secure within ourselves, we are grounded in

> When the heart goes before, like a lamp, and illumines the pathway, many things are made clear that else lie hidden in darkness.
>
> ·HENRY WADSWORTH LONGFELLOW·

love and no longer threatened by another's behavior. We are able to send love, rather than fear, into all situations.

A Course in Love explored in depth the power of love and how to awaken to its transformation and healing embrace. Here let us examine love not from the personal level, but from the Universal or impersonal level. We can say that love is impersonal because it is "no respecter of persons," and "it rains on the just and the unjust." This principle of Universal unity is available to all of us. We don't have to be "good enough" or kind enough to receive it.

Think of love as currents of electricity flowing through the wires in your home. When you go into a darkened room at night, you don't walk up to the light switch and try to convince it to go on because you've been a really good person that day. It would also not occur to you to get on your knees to beg and plead for it to flow. You simply flip the switch and the current runs into the bulb and the room is illuminated. The electricity is in your home because it is wired for electricity. Similarly, life is wired for love. You simply need to switch on your personal receptors. Not only is love available to us individually, but it is omnipresent, among families, groups, and communities, nationally and globally.

Not long ago I met a woman, Carolyn, a community peace activist concerned about a large international corporation that has extensive landholdings in her region. She believed the company to be self-serving, greedy, untrustworthy, aggressive, and dangerous and was of course troubled by its presence in the community. She viewed it as public enemy number one, and considered all the local people employed by the company as turncoats, as despicable as the company itself. The intensity of her loathing and anger disturbed me. Carolyn made it clear to me that she was "doing her part" to stop the company's aggression and was giving the "evil eye" to any of the "traitors" she encountered who worked for the corporation.

The Buddhist concept "Is this helpful?" sprang to my mind. Is this a helpful thing to do? Is this a helpful attitude? Obviously it was not. To attempt to combat what we perceive as aggression and disregard with seething aggression and disregard is *not* helpful. Whenever our actions come out of fear rather than love, they will mirror that fear. Carolyn's behavior illustrated the workings of a little mind, and, as *A Course in Miracles* tells us, little minds can be vicious. Frighteningly, they don't necessarily know they are being vicious. They are so ensnared in upside-down thinking that they see their actions as helpful, not exactly like those of the declared enemy.

Asking, "Is this helpful?" is a wonderful idea. Ask yourself:

Is this attitude helpful?
Is this behavior helpful?
Is this conversation helpful?
Is this judgment helpful?

When we ask such questions from our spiritual side, the answer will always remind us to return to love.

Love, Divine Universal Love, can heal the conflict felt in

> The heart of a wise man should resemble a mirror, which reflects every object without being sullied by any.
>
> ·CONFUCIUS·

Carolyn's community. Open minds and open hearts willing to meet in dialogue and exchange clear communication can prevent hostility. Love always shows the way. Love always has an answer. Love always *is* the answer. The enemy we see outside us is always a reflection of the enemy we hide within.

The following Buddhist technique is a good and mindful way to remind ourselves that what we see and judge as despicable outside us also lives within us.

Name the characteristics that you find bad or disagreeable in others, then add "just like me." If you are willing to see, the exercise will point out the uselessness of judgment in an instant. If Carolyn were willing to practice this technique, it would go like this:

They are self-serving—just like me. 

They are greedy—just like me.

They are untrustworthy—just like me.

They are aggressive—just like me.

They are hateful—just like me.

It's pretty easy to understand that what Carolyn "saw" in the corporation was what she didn't want to see about her own nature. Use the "just like me" technique and you will be amazed by several things: first, how judgmental you can be at times; second, how you have harbored some unkind and unloving feelings toward others and yourself; and third, how your judgmentalism decreases. The technique holds equally true for whatever we admire, respect, and love in other people: whatever good we behold in another must also live in us as well.

What a kind person she is—just like me.

What a generous man—just like me.

What a person of integrity—just like me.

Fortunately, in this case, it works both ways!

What are we to do as kind, loving people when we encounter social injustice, regional conflict, or lack of harmony at home or at the workplace? We must remember to connect with our love center and deal with the situation by sending love, rather than meeting aggression with aggression. Of course this is not an easy thing to do, but when we truly examine what our motivation is and what we want the results of this encounter to be, we can train ourselves to send love. Love has within it the seed of resolution. Meeting aggression with aggression can result only in intensified conflict and polarization.

Love Found on a 747

Not long ago, when my husband and I were flying from the Midwest to San Francisco, we were upgraded from coach to first class. After we boarded, the first-class cabin had two empty seats diagonally across from each other. Just as the door to the plane

> God wants the heart.
>
> ·TALMUD·

was closing, a young couple raced on, puffing from what must have been a mad dash through the airport to make their connecting flight. They were on their honeymoon, and obviously wanted to sit together.

David and I were the only couple in the cabin. The other passengers around us were all businessmen with their heads buried in work or *The Wall Street Journal.* Just as I was wondering how the flight attendant was going to handle the seating arrangements so the young couple could be together, she announced that the couple standing in the aisle had been married the day before and would very much like to sit next to each other. She asked if one of the gentlemen would be willing to change seats in order to accommodate the honeymooners.

If you could have heard the negative comments that ensued, you would not have believed your ears any more than I could believe mine. "Can you imagine having to sit next to your wife?" "Better sit together now, it won't last for long." "Just wait a few weeks, you'll want to sit at opposite ends of the plane." There were other comments that were equally appalling. I wanted to jump up and start preaching about love and holy relationships and share all kinds of spiritual wisdom. I turned to David and said in disgust, "I can't believe how negative these men are." He replied, "Just send them love, Joan." "I don't want to send them love," I snapped back. "I want to teach them that it's time they examined their negative attitudes, and that if they're in unhappy relationships it's no surprise to me, and . . ." "Just send them love," came David's voice. "Oh, all right," I reluctantly conceded, "but I still want to point out a thing or two."

I discreetly took several deep breaths and released my upset feelings and sent rays of love to everyone in the cabin. One man got up and sat in the empty seat behind David, so the honeymooners could snuggle in together. David and I kept sending love to all around, and a short while into the flight things began to change. The two men behind us closed their briefcases and started talking about their families and how much they missed them when they were traveling. When they commented about the pictures they were showing each other of their children and wives, I heard only loving words. Love transformed the negative energy in the cabin.

In any situation, we are coming from love or we are coming from fear. These are the only two emotions we are capable of expressing. Fear may take on many disguises—resentment, cyn-

When you make the two one,
and when you make the inner as the outer
and the outer as the inner
and the above as the below
and when you make the male and female
into a single one,
so that the male will not be male
and the female not be female . . .
then shall you enter the Kingdom.

·GOSPEL ACCORDING TO THOMAS·

> I and the Father are one.
>
> ·GOSPEL OF JOHN·

icism, rage, dishonesty, indifference, negativity—what lies underneath is always fear. Fear is unattractive, and inwardly we know it is in opposition to our Spiritual Reality. We project fear. We send it away from ourselves and then deny that what we see in another person could be what we harbor within ourselves. Fear always projects. Love, on the other hand, always extends. Love offers itself freely and totally wherever it is needed. Love has eyes that truly see and can look past fear to behold the truth of a person or situation. Love awakens us to a state of being alive, in which we honor and celebrate one another, when we see one another doing our best, "just like me." When we see someone missing the mark, we are no longer quick to condemn; we see ourselves and are quick to have compassion for that person.

I learned years ago that anything that isn't love is a cry for love. It's a tremendous Spiritual Principle to remember. The next time you observe someone exhibiting unskilled behavior, instead of condemning, practice sending love. The more we learn to come from love, the more our judgments drop away. Fear is banished from our consciousness and joy increases in our experiences as the natural by-product of love. Love as it is extended has many masks—or perhaps incarnations—as well. Love may appear as joy, kindness, passion, compassion, union, synergy, happiness, bliss, delight, and peace. These wonderful attributes are the results of the natural expression of love.

Love isn't something we acquire or even become; it is the very field of our being. We can become more loving as we become aware that we live, move, and experience our being alive in this field of being. The totality of Love in the Universe does not stop flowing because you do not see it. Love is available to us always. We must open our eyes to it. It flows through our thoughts, feelings, and bodies like water. Now we are capable of damming up the flow if we choose. If you think you have been doing so, here is an affirmation to work with:

> I, ___________, no longer resist love. I let it flow in and out of my life like water.

After repeating this several times, close your eyes and visualize love flowing in and out of your life. I find it helpful to visualize the flowing in and out with each beat of the heart. Love in, love out. On the outflow, release all that you have held on to that does not accord with this perfect love. Love in, love and all conflicted emotions and energies out. Love in, all else out. Love in, love out. After doing this for several minutes you'll begin to feel a deep sense of release and peace if you are truly letting go, followed by the warm glow of love. This is a helpful exercise to do if you are experiencing any kind of emotional or physical pain. Breathe the love in. Breathe the pain out until you begin to sense a release. Continue breathing, love in and love out.

Self-Love

Just as water seeks its own level—this is a principle of physics—so too does love seek its own level—this is a divine principle—and the level of love is always the highest imaginable.

If you feel a need for more love and loving relations in your life, focus your attention on giving rather than receiving love.

> His banner over me was love.
>
> ·SONG OF SONGS·

Begin right now to express more of the love that is in you. You can increase your awareness of the love that you have by spending time in meditation and focusing on the heart center and conscious love that is there. Allow it to grow and expand, sending it before you to bring unity and harmony into all of your encounters. This is something very practical that you can do, and for which you will receive positive results.

The following exercise is helpful as you learn to practice self-love.

A Week of Self-Love ✯

Day 1. Let positive acknowledgments sink in. When someone acknowledges you, listen, take a deep breath, and receive their acknowledgment. Then say, "Thank you."

Day 2. Give yourself a gift. Create a pleasure list of things to do or to have—and give yourself one gift from your list today.

Day 3. Stand naked in front of a full-length mirror, and tell yourself, "I love you," and what you like about what you see.

Day 4. Find something good about someone with whom you have a challenge, and then acknowledge the person.

Day 5. When someone complains to you, say you're sorry about the difficulty. Ask the person to tell you about something new and good in his or her life, and then listen.

Day 6. Do an anonymous "random act of kindness" for someone, and don't let it be known it was you.

Day 7. Spend one hour with a friend exchanging acknowledgments about yourselves, and love yourselves in each other's presence. If it becomes quiet, simply be with each other and enjoy that.

Practice written affirmations for the week.

I, ___________, like myself.

I, ___________, am a lovable person.

I, ___________, am now highly pleasing to myself.

I, ___________, am now highly pleasing to myself in the presence of others.

Create your own affirmations.

Set divine love in motion and all situations that are not harmonious will vanish! Nothing can resist the power of love. That is why we can say that love will dissolve all that is not in harmony. The more we can comprehend the power of love as the

> The cure for all the ills and wrongs, the cares, the sorrows, and the crimes of humanity, all lie in that one word "love." To each and every one of us, it gives the power of working miracles if we will.
>
> ·LYDIA CHILD·

moving force of the universe, the greater our loving experiences will be.

Charles Fillmore, cofounder of the Unity movement, wrote: "Love is the power that joins and binds in divine harmony the universe and everything in it; it is the greatest harmonizing principle known to man." Offer love and it will come to you, because love is always drawn to itself. If you offer attack, love will remain hidden, for it can live only in peace. Love is an inner quality that sees good everywhere and in everybody. Love insists that all is good, and by refusing to see anything but good it causes that quality to appear uppermost in itself and in all things. "The heart of him who truly loves is a paradise on earth, he has God in himself, for *God is Love.*" *God is Love* is a statement often repeated, and it has proven itself to be true. The biblical statement *God is Love* is perfectly accurate. God does not dole out love expecting it in return. God is love and you are the instrument of self-expression. To love God is to experience the feeling of love, to let love flow through you, to experience the opening of the heart center and the waves of energy that such an expansion brings. Love draws you closer and closer to God, to your good, to the point at which you are able to experience your being at one.

In Genesis we read: "Let us make man in our image and after our likeness." We are created after the image and likeness of the Father, which means that if God is Love, and He is, then so are we. A wonderful affirmation to work with:

Love created me like Itself.

Write it out on several cards. Carry one with you and place the others around your home and workplace. We all can learn about love by holding to this image of ourselves and releasing the mind from false images that preoccupy it much of the time.

Love created me like Itself.
Hear the truth about yourself in these words.
Love created me like Itself.
Love created me like Itself.

The flute of the infinite is played without ceasing
and its sound is love.

·KABIR·

Pay Attention to the Obvious

The Spiritual Law of Wisdom 8

The Wisdom of God is hidden within the depths of every soul. It is a priceless pearl, a thing of immeasurable value. We individually must discover and then use this remarkable gift. And when we do, this gift will prove itself to be our friend, guide, constant companion. It will show us the way, removing obstacles and providing guidance at every turn.

What, exactly, is this awesome gift? It is the realization that we are not now, and never have been, separate from our source—God. We may choose to live like orphaned children, but we are not. We are now and forever one with the Divine. Having free will, we are capable of denying this great truth as our personal reality, but we maintain our ignorance by this denial, which, according to *A Course in Miracles,* is "not to know." We cannot diminish the eternal Reality of Wisdom if we behave like

> Each one sees what he carries in his heart.
>
> ·JOHANN WOLFGANG VON GOETHE·

spiritual orphans. We are free to live in the misery of our own making, but we are not free to alter our true Spiritual Reality, that of beloved children who are one with their loving God. When we believe we are separate from God, we think He is separate from us, and our lives reflect painful experiences of that false belief.

When we awaken from such ignorant ways of thinking and living and realize what has always been true, our lives take on an exquisite purity, sweetness, and wonder.

The very idea of our invaluable worth is held forever in the mind of God. We are capable of uniting with God Mind, joining in consciousness to create the kind of life we have only dreamed of. Here we begin to experience miracles, to trust in the workings of a higher wisdom active in our lives. This wisdom is invaluable.

Of all the examples I know of God's having a better plan, this one will forever head the list.

Mabel Canon, an elegant woman I had known since childhood, had been married to her soulmate, Leonard, a dignified gentleman, for more than fifty years when she was diagnosed with cancer. Theirs was a deeply committed love, and they felt that together they could overcome the challenge of her illness.

They called me soon after Mabel was informed of her cancer. I went immediately to see them, and they described their years together and how blessed they felt. They recounted what they had lived through, including the death of their son Tom, who died at the young age of ten. They spoke of their involvement in the Unity Church; they had stopped attending services, however, when their minister took an assignment at Unity headquarters in Missouri. This was a surprise to me: I had no idea that these two charming people whom I had known casually, as older acquaintances of my parents', had been involved in the study of spirituality and metaphysics.

Enthusiastically I asked them, "What about Principle and Spiritual Law—have you continued to study the Principles?" They both looked at me blankly and replied, "Principles, what Principles?" I was stunned. How could two mature, intelligent adults who for a decade had attended the same church I used to attend ask this question? Well, I was to learn that Mabel and Leonard not only practiced the Principles but embodied them; they simply did not use the word in the same manner as I. They lived by the Principles, and in fact they became great teachers of mine.

The Canons asked whether I would be their minister and give them spiritual support through Mabel's illness. I had been ordained for perhaps a year and had no firsthand experience with someone in a quickly advancing cancerous condition. Mabel soon went into a hospital near my home, so almost every night I would visit for a few moments and pray with her. Leonard appeared to be holding up, and we all hoped for Mabel's recovery.

As the weeks passed, it became increasingly clear that our hopes were not going to be realized. Mabel would ask me to read inspirational material to her, and then she would suggest that perhaps it was time for her transition; maybe she would even see her beloved son Tom again. As her physical condition deteriorated, she seemed to be clinging more and more to the

> Each man must discover this Centre in himself, this Ground of his being, this Law of his life. It is hidden in the depths of every soul, waiting to be discovered. It is the treasure hidden in a field, the pearl of great price. It is the one thing that is necessary, which can satisfy all our desires and answer all our needs . . . It is the original Paradise from which we have come.
>
> ·BEDE GRIFFITHS·

physical. I was puzzled by this, and would lead her through meditations for the dying meant to assist them in letting go of the body. Still she held on, until her once beautiful body was nothing more than loose, gray skin over a skeletal frame. The more I spoke to her of letting go, the more she held on to the physical.

Meanwhile, Leonard, who had begun to feel poorly, went into a different hospital for tests. I tried to get him moved to the hospital where Mabel was, but was unsuccessful. When I visited him he seemed more troubled about being in the hospital than about being sick. A couple of weeks passed in which I saw Leonard twice a week; there was still no diagnosis of his condition. I continued to visit Mabel six nights a week. She appeared close to making her transition; she told me about seeing lights and angels in her room. When I would suggest that she join them, she would shake her head no, and that was that. Then deceased relatives joined her in the hospital room, and she related the fascinating details to me. One night Mabel sat up for the first time in more than a month and said, "Why, it's Tom,

Tom all grown up, can't you see him?" I could not, but quickly answered that perhaps she should go join him now. Not yet. The next night was Wednesday—the night I did not visit. Upon arriving home, around ten, I called the floor nurse to check on Mabel's condition. It was then that my intuition from earlier that evening was confirmed. Mabel had passed away quietly, alone, a few hours earlier. As I was processing this information, the nurse said, "Of course you must already know about Mr. Canon." "No," I replied, and she continued: "He unexpectedly died tonight, a short time before his wife."

This story still gives me "God bumps." This dear couple, married for fifty-four years, made their transitions the same night, several hours apart. Mabel knew what she was doing. No wonder she wasn't ready to let go. She was holding on with every last ounce of strength, waiting for her beloved to come and beckon her so they could enter the next dimension as they had always lived here . . . together. Oh yes, the Canons practiced Spiritual Law and lived it together until their last moments on this plane of existence and, I dare say, are living it in the next.

Mabel taught me how remarkably powerful our minds are. How there is a wisdom governing all of life that is beyond our comprehension. I was so inexperienced, so naive. The wisdom of Mabel's and Leonard's souls was so much more than I was able to grasp. With their passing on the same evening, I understood that they dwelled together in the mind of God. We all dwell in the infinite mind of God, yet often we do not remember this. Mabel and Leonard knew this truth on one level and their experience helped me learn it. The holy purpose for Mabel's holding on was beyond my ability to know, but it was always known within the mind of God.

> The Kingdom of Heaven is like unto a merchant man, seeking goodly pearls: who, when he had found one pearl of great price, went and sold all he had, and bought it.
>
> ·GOSPEL OF MATTHEW·

Our individual minds are forever a part of Divine Mind. This may not be the way you view yourself now, but it is the way that spiritualized "vision" will show you. Our individual minds can join consciously with Divine Mind and create, or our individual minds can appear to disconnect from Divine Mind and miscreate. Our creations are in alignment with goodness and love, and have life and substance to them. Our miscreations are out of alignment with everything and are fraught with conflict and struggle.

Let's do a little brainstorming exercise to move into a clearer understanding of the working of the Spiritual Law of Wisdom. Write on a sheet of paper:

"My mind is a part of God Mind; therefore the truth of me is that I am very holy."

Do you gasp at the very idea? Or do you humbly nod in agreement? The laws of the universe do not permit contradiction. Repeat silently with closed eyes:

"My mind is a part of God Mind; therefore the truth of me is that I am very holy."

Now search your mind for words to describe yourself. Include your ego-based attributes as well as the more spiritual ones, the positive as well as the negative. Write them as quickly as they come to you, and try not to judge.

Your list might look something like this:

I see myself as imposed upon.

I see myself as sad.

I see myself as angry.

I see myself as misunderstood.

I see myself as a good person.

I see myself as a moral person.

I see myself as blessed.

I see myself as living in integrity.

I see myself as loved.

I see myself as helpless.

I see myself as funny.

I see myself as controlling.

I see myself as a victim.

I see myself as worthless.

I see myself as undeserving.

I see myself as charitable.

I see myself as fortunate.

I see myself as intelligent.

I see myself as witty.

I see myself as desirable.

I see myself as priceless.

I see myself as irresistible.

When you complete your list, consider each negative attribute and comment on it, as in the following examples:

"I see myself as helpless, but the truth of my being is that my mind is a part of God's. I am very holy." Or, "I see myself as sad, but the truth of my being is that my mind is a part of God's. I am very holy." Sit for several moments with the above information. If related thoughts occur to you, write them too. You might add, "There is nothing my holiness cannot do."

This exercise is not about denying feelings. If you are desperate or very sad, you must deal with those feelings and process them. They are appropriate at certain times, but if the cause of such feelings is long past, it is time to move on.

The preceding writing assignment can be very helpful and powerful in the healing process. We all need to be reminded frequently of the truth of our being that is our foundation. As you endeavor to tap into the Spiritual Law of Wisdom, it is important to resist such self-defeating phrases as "I'm so confused" or "I don't know what to do." I know a person who says, "My mind is like a plate of mashed potatoes"—not a very attractive or inspiring image of self. Until we have made great strides forward in realizing our oneness with Divine Mind, we must be ever mindful to stop negative thoughts and expressions, and affirm only the mental and emotional state desired.

When in our spiritual growth we are able to grasp that our individual mind is not separate from Divine Mind but is a part of it, then we can extend our innate holiness to bless not only our lives but all life. This blessedness extends into our world. When

> The Tao [the Great Way] is priceless, a pearl containing Creation. In storage, it is utterly dark, without a trace. Brought out, its light shines through day and night. Becoming wise depends entirely on this—you need nothing else to be enlightened.
>
> ·LIU IMING·

we can see the world through our own holiness, we bless ourselves and the world together. Offer your holiness to everyone you meet. Simply by offering your holiness, simply by being willing to give it away, you keep it in your own awareness.

Divine Mind is made manifest in your world through the acceptance of your holiness. It can then be extended as rays of light, love, and blessings that enfold and uplift you and everyone who accepts your holiness. Our minds are holy and unlimited. Free of restrictions, the mind is mighty in its power to heal, bless, and uplift. You do not need to play small anymore. It does not serve you to play small, if you desire to acknowledge your holiness and your oneness with God. Accepting your holiness means the end of struggle, the end of guilt, and the end of hell. The guilt you have held in mind has made everything difficult for you. Acknowledging your holiness in your mind creates heaven on earth for you, here and now.

Embracing the Highest Answer

When we depart from our ego mind, we find that no matter what question or problem we are facing, there is a right and perfect answer, a right and perfect solution. When we are stuck in our ego mind this assertion seems laughable, if not insane. In our ego mind we see one another as competitors rather than as brothers and sisters. There are only winners and losers, and in order for us to win, someone else must lose. Life is played out on a battlefield. We will win some battles and lose others, we will at some time be counted among the wounded. But there is another way to live on this planet: to engage fully in our lives, and still think with our higher mind, which is forever a part of Divine Mind. Here's an example of thinking—and living—with our higher mind.

Joe's wife, Maria, had died young, of a rare blood disease, leaving him to bring up their young daughter alone. Jennifer was eleven when her mother died, and she was devastated. Joe and Jennifer had intensive grief counseling for a few years. At fourteen Jennifer seemed well adjusted. She was doing well in school and pursuing her interest in equestrian sports. She had even talked her dad into buying her a horse. Joe was a devoted father, trying to be both father and mother for his daughter and managing a rapidly expanding computer parts business.

Everything looked fine, but then Jennifer began cutting school, lying, not caring for her horse. Joe was angry and confused. He tried controlling Jennifer's free time, and her choice of friends. She would sneak out her bedroom window and spend time with an older, tough crowd. She began to drink heavily and use drugs, which she obtained from a twenty-year-old "boyfriend."

When Joe learned this, he was crushed. He had endured the loss of his wife, but he could not endure the loss of his daughter. I met Joe and Jennifer around this time. She was sullen and withdrawn, refusing to communicate with her father or me. Joe's pain was so intense that when I invited him to tell Jennifer what he felt, I filled up with tears. He loved his daughter and wanted

> I believe that God is in me as the sun in the colour and fragrance of a flower—the Light in my darkness, the Voice in my silence.
>
> ·HELEN KELLER·

to protect her from pain, and here she was, creating anguish for herself and her father.

I used a counseling technique that involves withdrawing from what is being said and tuning into what lies underneath, so that what is not being said will be expressed. Two spiritual principles came into my consciousness, both related to the Universal Laws of Mind.

1. We are never upset solely for the reason we think.
2. Children often act out their parents' unresolved problems.

I was not sure how these two principles related to the dynamic between Jennifer and her dad, so I just put these ideas out on the table. I asked that we consider how they might apply. Jennifer and Joe began to think about the first statement. They wrote it out and then listed possible reasons for being upset.

Joe wrote: "I'm never upset only for the reason I think. I think I'm upset because of Jennifer's behavior. Her grades are declining, she's not caring for her horse, she's running with the wrong crowd. Then there's her boyfriend, her drinking, drugs, and the lying." Then he wrote: "If all this is not the real reason I'm upset, what could it be? I'm upset that I'll lose Jennifer like I lost Maria. I'm upset that I've lost control. I'm upset . . ."

I read his list and asked him, "What's underneath all this,

what's lurking within?" Joe broke down and sobbed, touching a well of grief that he had kept barricaded for four years. "We are never upset for the reason we think" led Joe to uncover a deep layer of grief he carried around all the time. When Jennifer, acting out her father's unhealed pain, created so much surface pain for herself and for him, their misery was cracked wide open. Now the necessary healing for father and daughter could begin. Jennifer's demeanor changed immediately. The expression in her face and eyes softened. She started to cry and express all that she had kept locked in her heart. Father and daughter, both in tears, embraced. Soon I too was crying, as I felt their love for each other and their first steps on the road to healing.

Parents seldom welcome the thought that their troubled teen's behavior has something to do with them. Those who are willing to look deeply can find much insight here. We are always drawing players into the script of our lives to point out what needs to be healed in us. What better actors to play that role for us than our children?

"I'm never upset only for the reason I think" is one of the best one-line exercises to gain insight into what is really going on in any situation. I think I'm upset because you're always late, but I'm really upset because of my own unresolved abandonment issues. I think I'm upset because you're a sloppy dresser, but I'm really upset because people will think that I have no control and that I must be a slob as well. I think I'm upset because I have a demanding boss, but I'm really upset because I carry so many unresolved authority issues.

Pay Attention to the Obvious

Many of us believe life has to be complicated and if we are to receive Divine direction, it will be very subtle, even obscure. But

> I am closer to you than yourself,
> Than your soul, than your own breath.
> Why do you not see me?
> Why do you not hear me?
>
> ·IBN AL-ARABIX ARABI·

that direction isn't far from view at all. Years ago, my husband and I learned something from a spiritual teacher that continues to serve us: "Pay attention to the obvious."

Think of the old story about the man who goes to the doctor and says, "It hurts when I do this." The doctor responds, "Then don't do that." We must practice reading the road signs as we journey through life, and as I've discovered, they are pretty obvious. If you try to open a door again and again and it won't budge, try another door! Remember, life isn't a struggle. What is best for you to do is not hidden; it's always in plain view. You just need to see it.

There are many subtle messages along the path of life, and tuning in to them is important. But the life-changing signs are always right in front of us, and we only have to remember: "Pay attention to the obvious."

A Course in Miracles teaches: "The outstanding characteristic of the *laws* of mind as they operate in the world is that by obeying them, and I assure you, that you must obey them, you can arrive at diametrically opposed results." What you hold in your mind and project on another person or on the world you believe to be so, to be true, and to that extent it is so. When we reach through the power of Mind the highest spiritual thoughts, we make the right choice because we are tuned in to the wisdom of Divine guidance. In this state of mind we cease attempting to force an issue or enforce our will. We listen and follow the wisdom of God and not only walk the right path, but also discover it is the easy path. Remember always, struggle is of the ego, ease is of the Spirit.

Follow the right path, and learn it is also the easiest path. People ask, "How can I tell if I am doing the right thing or going in the right direction and making the correct choice?" The answer is simple. Ask yourself, "Am I happy? Do I *feel* good, and are things flowing with ease?" If you can answer yes, then thoughts from the center of Wisdom have transformed you. If you're not feeling good and happy, you may want to review your thoughts and feelings to see if you have been demanding, judgmental, headstrong, or imposing your will. We all receive guidance about what to do next, how to proceed with the living of our lives. Some people choose to listen and others choose not to. The power of Divine Wisdom supports, guides, and sustains us, and will provide for the future. When Wisdom is quickened we need take no thought for the future, but only keep our minds clear to receive the messages of Wisdom.

Help Me Lift This Heavy Load

The Spiritual Law of Non-Attachment

9

We will experience a natural resonance and ease with some Spiritual Laws, and with others we will know they hold a great truth, but a truth that our soul must really work on. We must see what lessons we individually are here to learn.

The idea of non-attachment initially caused me personal discomfort. In our materialistically driven Western society there is a tremendous value placed on ownership. From an early age we are collectively given the message that we must own a car, then a home, then a better car, more cars, a better home, nice things, land, stocks, bonds—and on and on we own and own.

Of course, once we own something, we then must spend time caring for it. We are concerned with its current value, its depreciation or appreciation. We spend from minutes to hours every day thinking about our things. Even children are taught this way

> Cultivate holy boldness, for God helps the strong.
>
> ·ST. TERESA·

of living: four-year-olds want certain logos on their clothing, because it's the in thing among the preschool set. We mature into people driven to accumulate. Soon, if we are not extremely careful, we no longer own our home, cars, stocks, bonds, all our things. They own us.

"Whoever dies with the most toys wins": Perhaps this tongue-in-cheek comment will make you pause and reflect on your life and its true value. How ludicrous to believe that what we own establishes who we are. Many believe this, but it couldn't be further from the truth. In the ultimate sense no one can ever own anything. We are only temporary custodians of our possessions.

The impossibility of lasting ownership dawned clearly in my understanding the first time I was on the island of Hawaii, soon after David and I were married. On a gorgeous sunny day, we went for a drive to see where a new lava flow from Mauna Loa had spilled into the sea and was forming additional land. I was excited at the prospect of witnessing how Mother Earth reproduces herself through volcanic activity. We were going to observe in that moment evidence of the same activity that has been occurring for eons, the process that formed the entire Hawaiian chain.

What we saw upon arriving near this recently formed earth were makeshift signs posted on recently cooled lava: "No Trespassing—Private Property." I started to chuckle and then began to laugh louder and louder, until I was holding my sides. I'm sure David thought his bride was going over the edge. When

I saw those signs on a lava flow that now covered what a few months earlier had been ocean, I had a moment of absolute insight. I saw not only how silly that notion was, but how silly the idea of any ownership was.

Can we own any piece of the earth? We can believe we do, but it is really a childish concept. When we can look insightfully into the illusion of ownership, it is easy to become non-attached to any of our possessions. There is nothing wrong with having "stuff"; it's always our attachment to it that leads us astray.

Life is transitory. We cannot get around that fact. Nothing that is physically here now will last forever. Even some of the stars we see at night may have died long ago.

With increased understanding of the transitory nature of things comes the increased ability to be non-attached, not only to things, but people and outcomes as well. When we are non-attached, we can surrender to the present moment and trust that the Wisdom of the Universe will work in concert with our own inner wisdom to bring into our lives what is necessary for that moment to be blessed.

Let us look at the process from the viewpoint of energy. When we are in a possessive state of mind, be it possessive of things, ideas, or people, our energy is rigid, solidified, nonflowing, restrictive. That rigidity shows up as stuck energy in our body and consciousness, which results in stuck situations in our lives. In order for energy to work efficiently and effectively, it must be unrestricted, free-flowing. When we are non-attached to things, people, and outcomes, the energy of life flows freely through our lives and creates in every moment what is ideal for us.

If you are someone who likes to be in control, this principle will not be easy for you. When you attempt to control, you limit most of your possibilities for abundance and good.

Giving up control, practicing non-attachment, and surrendering to a higher divine plan—this is not a simple undertaking for most of us. We must lay aside our early programming of "ownership" and shift our thinking to being guardians or temporary caretakers of things or people.

Kahlil Gibran, in his poem "On Children," says: "Your children are not your children. They are the sons and daughters of life longing for itself." Some parents have a difficult time releasing the concept of ownership of their children. But as they grow into teenagers and from teenagers into adults, it is clear, sometimes laughably so, that any attempt at ownership and control of them is an exercise in futility.

Non-attachment and surrender bring us into alignment with the natural abundance of life. Years of carrying the burden of making things happen cause us to be weary and tired. Struggling endlessly is the way of the ego. Surrendering, flowing, and allowing the Universe to support us is the way of the soul in tune with the Spirit. Letting the Universe handle the details means giving up control, trusting that God can actually be God in a particular situation in your life. When we exclaim a resounding yes to our higher purpose at any given moment, all of life rushes in to support us. What I have discovered through years of practice is that the more quickly I can let go, the quicker Spirit can get going.

Letting the Universe handle the details does not mean hiding all day under the covers; it does mean we are guided to do one thing: make a contact that leads to a positive connection, and make a contact that leads to the next step. Something better than we have imagined will inevitably occur. Sometimes we are afraid to let the Universe handle the details, afraid that if we relinquish control the little bit of good we do have will be lost or taken from

> Scripture says, "No one knows the Father but by the Son." Therefore, if you want to know God, you must not only be like the Son, you must be the Son.
>
> ·MEISTER ECKHART·

us, and that then things will be worse and we will have nothing. Because of this fear we hold on too long to a few crumbs while the Universe is busy baking us a magnificent celebratory cake.

Practice writing the following affirmations, inserting your own first name in the blanks. Do each one until you can affirm "Yes!" Then move to the next.

It is safe for me, ____________, to surrender.

It is safe for me, ____________, to let go.

It is safe for me, ____________, to let go of control.

The more quickly I, ____________, let go of control, the more quickly I enter the flow.

I, ____________, let go, and I enter the flow.

The Universe loves to support my grandest dreams.

To let the Universe handle the details is one of the greatest lessons we can learn, and one of the most powerful. When we allow the Universe to handle the details we can only gain. Loss of any kind is impossible. Letting the Universe handle the details means that you are willing to put the ego aside and trust that you are loved and that you will be cared for. You matter to God.

As we step aside, at first very hesitantly, later with increased confidence, we are allowing the truth of our being to precede us and clear the way, to draw to us exactly what is needed at *any* given moment.

Barbara had recognized years ago that she was by nature a very controlling person, clinging to everything—her husband, children, parents, and friends, money and other possessions. She was aware of how her control was blocking the free flow of Universal energy and causing her much upset and little satisfaction. She was always stressed and tense.

For one month Barbara practiced a mindfulness breathing technique that greatly assisted her in releasing control and surrendering to the present moment. What she did, you too can do effectively.

Each time Barbara felt the urge to control, she made herself aware of how that grasping energy felt within her body. She would stop whatever she was doing and take slow, deep breaths in and out—breathing in surrender, breathing out control. Then she would breathe slowly and deeply into the present moment and exhale slowly, consciously smiling as she breathed out.

Here's the technique, step by step:

> Do the following three times: Breathe in deeply and slowly. Be aware of breathing in surrender. Breathe out fully and slowly. Be aware of breathing out control.
>
> Then do the following three times: Breathe in deeply and slowly into the present moment. Breathe out fully and slowly into the present moment.
>
> Think: "And I smile and it's a wonderful moment." Then smile.

Practice this gentle technique daily, even if you do not have control to release. It will remind you to live in the present moment, which is the only moment there is.

When we step aside we can be certain that truth will go before us, leading the way. You may find it helpful to practice letting the Universe handle the details by removing those nagging fear thoughts that say "No way!" These are some helpful affirmations:

> I enjoy allowing the Universe to handle the details.
>
> The more I, ___________, allow the Universe to handle the details, the freer I am.
>
> The more I, ___________, allow the Universe to handle the details, the better my life works.

When we live under the mistaken belief that we must "do it alone," we place ourselves under tremendous strain, both physically and spiritually. In recent months I have met many women around the country who have told me about their deep and haunting depressions. Most were dependent on medication, and uneasy with this dependence. Not one said she was happier as a result of such therapy. Without exception, these women seemed deeply sad, without hope, and saw no way out. No one had spoken to them about their spiritual life, about nurturing their inner spirit, their soul.

Diane, a nurse for twenty years, was one of the women I talked to. She had recently completed her master's degree and was doing in-home care for AIDS patients during the last months of their lives. She was turning nearly all of her earnings over to her husband to assist him with alimony payments and child

> Fuss, god of the Southern Ocean, and Fret, god of the Northern Ocean, happened once to meet in the realm of Chaos, god of the Center. Chaos treated them very well and they discussed how to repay him. They had noticed that, where everyone has seven apertures, for sight, hearing, eating, breathing, Chaos had none. So they decided to make the experiment of boring holes in him. Every day they bored a hole, and on the seventh day Chaos died.
>
> ·CHUANG-TZU·

support and college tuition for his first family. As a result, Diane, who used to enjoy pampering herself with regular massages, monthly facials, manicures, and elegant clothes, was doing nothing for herself. There were no longer lunches out with colleagues and friends, no weekend retreats. There were no rewards to herself to ease the stress of long hours of intense work and the additional stress of taking on her husband's responsibilities, after years of being on her own, and responsible to and for herself alone.

Diane was constantly sacrificing and struggling, doing without and reaping very little. No wonder she was depressed. I encouraged her to have a heart-to-heart talk with her husband, whom she loves very much, to come from her center and speak her truth. She should not ask him for permission to restructure their financial lives, I told her, for this would place her in the role of child while her husband would be assuming the role of parent.

Such positioning, although frequent between them, would be unhealthy for both.

Diane was instructed to state to her husband that the current arrangement no longer worked for her and actually had never worked for her. She had gone along with them for the past several years only to try to ease his burden, but she could no longer support his daughter, who was living on more money per month than she. I taught her to say simply, "This does not work for me," rather than tell him he was wrong or was giving too much out of guilt. When we communicate, "This does not work for me," we reclaim our power and use our inner strength to support ourselves rather than fall back on the role model of victim.

Diane gave her power and her paycheck away. She gave her sense of well-being over to another person. This is never a good idea, whether that other person is husband, wife, parent, child, colleague, friend, or boss, or an agency or organization. Diane had to reclaim her power and strength, and once she did that, she had to find a way to fit God into the equation of her life. With her depression and exhaustion, she had Eased God Out.

EGO: Easing God Out

This is what the ego self does: it forever relies on its strength to ease God out of the equation. When this happens, we see ourselves as insignificant and vulnerable. We have every reason to be afraid, because we have attempted to usurp the power of God, to impose our tiny will over the magnificent all of the Will of God. The ego in us believes that each time it eases God out of some aspect of life it has bettered itself. It is always competitive rather than loving, substituting chaos and conflict for meaning

The ultimate Path is without difficulty.
Just avoid picking and choosing.

·SEING-TS'AN·

and harmony, complexity for simplicity, damnation for forgiveness. When we allow it to, the ego can ease God out of the framework of our life. The results are exhaustion, depression, a haunting uneasiness—a life out of balance.

Spirit, Soul, Body

We are threefold beings—spirit, soul, body. Individually we have our own bodies and souls, but together we share one spirit. In order for our individual expression of life to flow and work in harmony, each of these three areas must be attended to, nurtured, and gently brought into balance.

Our spirit is forever one with God. It is perfect, eternal, changeless, unalterable. Our spirit is always co-creating with the Creator, and always knowing of our perfection; it cannot be altered by any actions, no matter how meritorious or how unskilled. Spirit remains complete, free, and immortal. Spirit cannot be divided or compartmentalized. It is limitless. It is one. The reality of Spirit is expressed this way in *A Course in Miracles:* "Against this sense of temporary existence, spirit offers knowledge of permanence and unshakable being." Spirit is pure creative energy vibrating at the highest frequency. When we are attuned to the spirit within ourselves and live from this true self, we extend Divine Energy into the world.

Soul, the second part of our threefold nature, is the aspect that is our unique psyche, our individual and personal expression

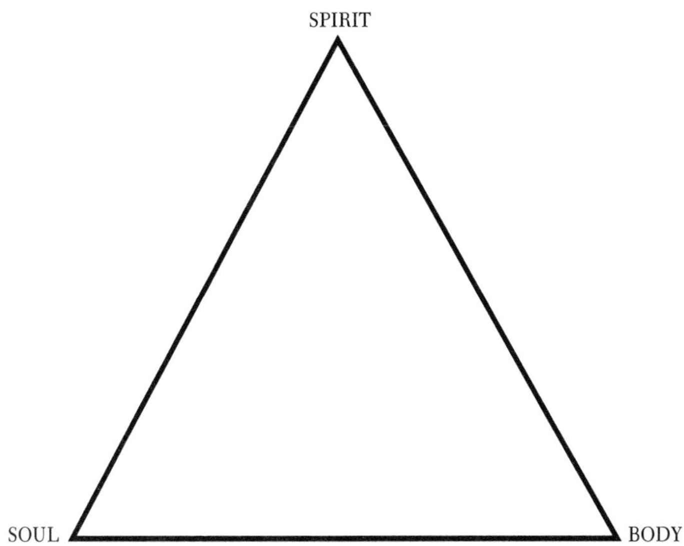

of God energy. Soul is what makes the inward you *you*. The soul draws forth its information from the realm of spirit, as well as from the physical realm. The soul is pivotal, turning at times toward the spirit and at times toward the body or physical world to gather information. All of life's experiences become encoded on the soul. We can sully the soul and need to purify it; in this sense it differs from the spirit, which forever remains perfect. The energy vibrating at the level of soul is invisible, but beginning to take form.

The third aspect of our nature is the body, whose formed energy is the densest of all. The body functions in the physical realm and is often ruled by the demands of the ego, becoming its servant. The body can serve a much higher purpose, as we consciously lift it into the journey of spirit and have healing be its new direction. Always remember: You *have* a body; you *are not* your body. Your body is a tiny aspect of the entirety of your reality, which is a glorious, free—and enormous—spiritual being.

It is crucial that we be fully engaged in our own well-being. This ensures that we balance spirit, soul, and body. When one aspect is out of balance, the others are also out of balance, and we are at risk. If our Spirit is not nurtured it becomes, as far as we would be aware, withered, starving for nourishment, attention, and respite. We diminish in situations like this, not only in Spirit, but also in body or soul or both. All three aspects must be in balance.

An example of imbalance can be seen in cases of alcoholism. The alcoholic drinks to drown a deep soul wound or a withered spirit. To avoid the pain on the soul level, he pollutes the physical form with alcohol, thus depleting the immune system, damaging the liver, and destroying all possibility of a healthy relationship. Not only does the disease of alcoholism affect the body, it is the effect of deep problems ignored on the other two levels of being. The only programs that can treat alcoholism effectively—indeed, the only programs that can treat any disorder effectively—must treat man's threefold nature. For any true and lasting healing, we must see ourselves as threefold beings, spirit, soul, and body, rather than only body.

I have a body. I am not my body.

This is a great affirmation to work with in coming to understand the distinction between having and being.

I may have a new car. I am not my new car.

I may have a new home. I am not my new home.

I may have a cold. I am not the cold.

I may have the disease of alcoholism. I am not the alcoholism.

You are never the disease or illness, for all disease and illness are temporary conditions, while you are an eternal idea in the mind of God.

When we bring body and soul in alignment with spirit, we are aligned with God. We experience the ultimate ease of resting in God, which is the destination of surrender and the manifestation of fully practicing the Spiritual Law of Non-Attachment.

The Prosperity Principle

The Spiritual Law of Abundance 10

We live in a remarkably abundant universe. A much-misunderstood and most important Spiritual Principle is that the very nature of life is abundant, and we are intended to live it abundantly. As Auntie Mame exclaims, in a line I've always loved, "Life is a banquet and most poor suckers are starving to death." Yes, life is a banquet, a lavish, opulent banquet, and in order to enjoy all the delicacies on the buffet table, we have to get up, go to the table ourselves, and fill our own plates. And in order to get up and go to the buffet table, we first must feel worthy to be in the banquet hall. We must feel deserving. We must abandon our scarcity consciousness, any belief system that focuses on lack and limitation.

When we are living with a scarcity consciousness, no matter what opportunities are offered us, what is given to us, it is never enough, or we are so blind we do not even see the gifts. We always see the glass as half empty. In fact, with a scarcity con-

> Everything comes from your own heart. This is what one ancient called bringing out the family treasure.
>
> ·YUAN-WU·

sciousness we focus so much on the emptiness that that becomes all we can see.

Most of us have experienced the scarcity principle at some time in life. It is a terrifying position from which to live. We are forever in fear that what few crumbs we do have will be snatched from us at any moment. What little we have seems to be slipping through our fingers and our lives.

I have known multimillionaires who live with a scarcity consciousness. No matter how much they own, it is never enough; deep within they are afraid that at any moment all they have can be torn from them. They feel a lack inside, and no amount of exterior wealth can fill that inner emptiness.

The Abundance Principle, like all Spiritual Principles, has to be recognized and practiced in order to integrate it fully into daily living. As we develop this consciousness of abundance as our divine heritage, we attract into our lives whatever good we desire. Note I said "attract," yet not through physical exertion, not through struggle or sacrifice, but through right of consciousness. When consciousness is attuned to abundance, outer manifestations of that inner consciousness can be drawn into our lives.

This doesn't mean you don't have to work for the fulfillment of your desires, but it does mean you no longer have to struggle for them. When we have to struggle for anything, it's a sign that we are relying on our strength alone and have left the spirit out of the equation. Whenever some project or endeavor becomes difficult in my life, I know that the project or the timing is not right, and I immediately let it go.

Living the abundant life means recognizing struggle and scarcity thinking, and giving them up immediately. Replace the limited thoughts with ideas of abundance and plenty.

The Four Aspects of Abundance

There are four main aspects to the Law of Abundance:

1. Blessing
2. Giving
3. Receiving
4. Accepting

These are like the four sides of a square; all of them must be practiced and kept in balance in order to embrace the law fully. We will now explore each of them in depth.

Blessing

This is the first side of the abundance square.

We can acknowledge what we already have by the act of blessing it. We can engage in the simple act of counting our personal blessings and giving thanks for each one.

Here are some suggestions for you: Look to your inner life, family, friends, career, interests, talents, and passions, and give thanks for them individually and collectively. Focus on what you already have with a grateful heart. For every accomplishment and good that enters your life, consciously give thanks. For each positive, progressive step you take in your life, give thanks.

If you desire a new computer, give thanks for and bless your old PC. If you want a new or better job, constantly bless your current one. When you've worked hard and long to accomplish a task or realize a dream, give thanks and bless the situation or dream come true.

Blessing and giving thanks automatically increase whatever good you are receiving. Practice daily blessings, on your family, home, furniture, trees, car, airplanes, strangers on the highway, clerks, agreeable *and* disagreeable people. Bless all situations, and harmony and abundance will be established and will increase in your life.

Giving

This is the next side of the abundance square.

When we recognize that we live in an abundant world, we know that we indeed have what is necessary to fulfill us—happiness, security, plenty of the good we want. We naturally have the desire to share in this knowledge, and the most noticeable way to do this is through giving.

Each time we give, we are actually proving to ourselves that we have. Think about it. If you believe you are impoverished, you could hardly entertain the idea of giving. When you know you come from abundance, giving is the most natural thing in the world.

There are many levels of giving. We give of ourselves through our willingness to listen or pay attention to others, we give with a kind word or note or letter, we give by volunteering our time or talent, we give by sharing our wealth with our church or temple, the arts, or another cause dear to our hearts. We give each time we are generous or gracious.

I have a friend who finds such joy in giving that her friends have become very mindful about paying her compliments. I have seen her take off a very expensive one-of-a-kind sweater and

> The fruit drops when it is ripe.
>
> ·ZEN SAYING·

give it to an admiring friend. For Christmas one year she gave me a Chanel bag she had been carrying. It had caught my eye, and I had complimented her on how beautiful it was. She has given away a fur coat and beautiful jewelry, and in her giving she is always gracious. She also regularly tithes to her church. She loves to give, and through giving she is always enriching her spiritual treasure chest.

When people ask me how much they should give, I say, "Give until it feels good." The idea "Give until it hurts" is, I think, the wrong way to approach it. To develop your giving muscles, I don't suggest you start by giving away any possession of yours that someone compliments you on. Begin where you are, and take consistent and gradual steps.

A good starting point is to be generous with your spirit. Take notice of something good or noteworthy every day. Whether you are at home, at your workplace, with friends, colleagues, or family, give a sincere compliment, share your appreciation and praise. We can all give by generously sharing our thoughtfulness, attention, and time with loved ones and those in need.

Share with those who come into your life or your awareness with a request. I view all such encounters not as chance but rather as divine design. Does this mean we are always to give to those who ask? Yes, it does. It also means you can choose whether you give your money, your time, or simply an acknowledging nod and, "Sorry, not today."

Many people have described to me their internal conflict in

dealing with people panhandling on the street. Some express disgust at the street person's life and righteously speak of never acknowledging them or giving them anything, "which only encourages them to beg." Apparently these people feel God has set up the haves to be judge and jury for the have-nots. Having or not having is only temporary, and neither condition makes us any more precious to God Mind.

The next time someone asks you for a quarter or a dollar, examine your feelings. What's the big deal if you give? It will make no difference in your finances, and maybe it will soften your heart. In such circumstances I always consider what Jesus would do, what the Buddha would do. I can hardly imagine those holy ones saying, "What a despicable being! Don't bother me!"

Give generously when you are asked, for you may have encountered angels unaware.

Find ways to give lovingly from your essence in all situations. You thereby become the blessing, and as the law works, you will be blessed in return.

Friends of mine who are very creative have some interesting ways to deal with the matter of street people and panhandlers. Chandler, a successful financial planner, was in New York City on business for a week. Each morning when he left his hotel, he saw the same panhandler, and he gave him a warm greeting. After a few mornings of this routine, Chandler shared with this man an idea that had occurred to him: he asked the man if he was game for a little financial experiment. The man said he was interested, so Chandler went to his room, found a piece of cardboard, and on one side wrote in bold letters:

FINANCIAL ADVICE

50 CENTS

He turned the cardboard over and wrote a quick message on the other side.

Chandler then went back to the man on the street and presented him with the freshly made sign. Chandler instructed the man not to turn the sign over until he had the fifty-cent payment in his hat. Then, and only then, was the "investor" to receive the financial advice:

BUY LOW

SELL HIGH

Chandler left for his morning business, returning a few hours later to see the man grinning broadly with several people gathered around him. He had been giving his advice so successfully that morning that he had earned more than twenty dollars. He had an expanded sense of worth, and he was having fun. Chandler felt that in a small way he had made a difference in the man's life.

Another friend of mine, Bert, lives a life of true abundance. When visiting a city where he is likely to encounter people asking for a handout, Bert starts the day with five new ten-dollar bills in an outer pocket. The first five people who ask him for money are each given ten dollars. Bert tells the story of being in San Francisco when a man approached him and asked for a quarter. Bert handed him a ten-dollar bill, and the astonished man thanked him and walked away. After taking a few steps he turned and called to Bert, "Hey, mister, are there any more where this came from?"

It is vitally important to give a portion of our money away, without strings, to the place where we receive our spiritual nourishment. If you have no place of spiritual nourishment, you

> Ask and it shall be given you; seek and ye shall find; knock and it shall be opened unto you.
>
> ·GOSPEL OF MATTHEW·

need to find one. Even the most enlightened of us needs a place where soul and spirit are nourished and filled.

There are few of us without a need for more money. Receiving additional cash in our lives is no different from receiving more of anything else. We must *give* first. Many people can consider giving their money to God's work only as a sort of barter: God, you do thus and so, and I'll give *x* amount of money to my church or synagogue or to the poor in India. These are ego promises, and this is not true giving. It is often a veiled attempt to manipulate the universe. This is giving as the ego interprets giving, not as the spirit understands it. We might call such misguided giving "giving to get."

There is an ancient story of an Eastern disciple who was traveling without financial resources. Finding himself penniless, he prayed, "Oh Lord, help me. Please let me find some money, and if I do, I vow to you I shall immediately go to the temple and make a fine offering."

Almost instantly he found a valuable coin partially hidden by the dust on the road. The disciple was excited, and he thanked God for his good fortune. As he resumed walking he began to reconsider his vow. Soon he was thinking he had been too hasty and generous when he made that vow. Why, that coin was there in the road all along, he thought; I should have waited.

Upon entering the next town, he went directly to the money changer, who carefully examined the old coin and then told the disciple he could give him only seventy-five percent of the coin's value because of its worn condition. Annoyed, the disciple took his money and left the money changer's. When he was outside he looked skyward and said, "How very clever of you, Lord, to take your portion here, since I became unwilling to give it to you as I promised."

TITHING—PLAYING WITH THE BIG KIDS

A favorite line of mine in *A Course in Miracles* tells us: "Into the hands that give, the gift is given." When we move into more conscious levels of living, we become aware of an actual need to give. In all of our giving, I believe, we *must* give money. Nothing starts bringing up and clearing out our money issues like giving it away.

There is an expression in spiritual thought: "The Universe demands its ten percent." Is there something mystical or magical about ten percent? Some say yes, it's an ancient biblical teaching of returning one-tenth back to God, be it land, cattle, crops, or money. Some say no, there's nothing special about ten percent. What I know to be universally true about giving ten percent is that you notice it!

Let's say you have a thousand dollars, and you give five. That five dollars is not a significant amount in your life. It is not even tip money, not an amount that your soul wakes up and takes notice of. On the other hand, if out of a thousand dollars you give a hundred to the place where you receive spiritual nourishment, you will notice that hundred dollars moving elsewhere. When we consistently engage in such a high level of giving, we are acknowledging and affirming how much has already been given to us and how blessed we are.

Ten percent, whether you're dealing with $100, $1,000,

$10,000, $100,000, or $1 million, is noticeable. It is an amount that enters you fully into the abundance game. I see giving ten percent and more as a sacred activity. I've been a tither (giving ten percent to my church home) for well over twenty years, and I have always found that the more abundance I shovel out, the more God keeps shoveling back into my life. The amazing part is that God always has a bigger shovel.

Consistently giving a tithe means consistently and actually putting God first in our life. Many people live life so much out of their wallets and bank accounts that it takes them a real shift in consciousness to be able to give at such a high level. When we freely, willingly, joyously give ten percent:

1. The remaining ninety percent goes farther than the hundred percent ever did.
2. New avenues of abundance and financial opportunities are constantly opening.
3. All fears of money—of not having enough—evaporate.
4. We have clearly put what is important first.
5. We acknowledge God as our source.

Almost daily I affirm, "God is my Source." The ministry is not my source, the lectures and workshops I give are not my source, my books are not my source. Giving ten percent to where God is nurturing me affirms my conviction. It is fun, it is a joy, and it is a miracle-working power in my life, and countless other people's lives as well. Once we prime our "giving pump," we find more ways to be generous with one another, and we find our joy steadily increasing.

At a recent dinner I attended with a highly visible author, the subject of giving came up. He shared that over the years, with his increased success, he has been able to share his good fortune with many loved ones in significant ways. He has bought and paid for seven homes, for his mother, his brothers, and his wife's siblings. He has bought and given away twenty-five new cars. I asked him what that felt like. He responded simply that it felt very good. I would love to be able to give like that, wouldn't you?

Well, we must practice giving right where we are—now. If we are mentally and emotionally locked from the giving department, we must move that stuck energy by opening our minds, hearts, souls, and checkbooks.

Following is a list of my preferred techniques to start abundance muscles working and develop prosperity consciousness.

1. Stop paying with change. That means that if your bill is $6.17, give the clerk seven dollars or a ten- or twenty-dollar bill. Don't focus your energy, time, and consciousness counting out seventeen cents. Start to shift your thinking and think big.
2. Whenever you have an opportunity to give, *give*. This means putting something in the March of Dimes container at the grocery checkout or the Salvation Army pot at Christmas, or buying a box of cookies from a Girl Scout. When the baskets of life are passed, don't hesitate, *give*.
3. Each time you see your paper money in your wallet or on a table, look at the "In God We Trust" side. Seeing this reaffirms your trust in God as your Source. Take a large bill, a fifty or a hundred, fold it so you can see the denomination, and put it in your wallet so you can see it daily. In this way you will always have fifty or a hundred

dollars with you to remind yourself regularly you have resources immediately available. This helps you feel prosperous.

4. Frequently do something generous for a loved one, without any expectations. Participate at a level that works for you now. It doesn't have to be buying someone a home—perhaps just lunch.
5. Notice the abundance of the Universe all around you, and appreciate and feel the richness of life. See the beauty in a child's eyes. Experience the birth of new green in spring or the blaze of color in autumn. Lie under the stars on a clear night and drink in the wonder. Walk through the woods, stroll on the beach, or sit by a quiet lake and communicate with the Infinite.
6. Never say, "I can't afford . . ." Change your thinking to: "I choose to put my money elsewhere right now."
7. Discard any tattered possessions: clothing, household items, or other things that scream lack and poverty consciousness.
8. If you have not used something in two years, you can live without it. Sell it, or better yet, give it away.
9. Notice the abundance in your life. Write a list.
10. Give without strings.
11. Give until it feels good.
12. If you want to move up to experiencing incredible abundance, start tithing (ten percent of your gross income) wherever you receive your spiritual food.
13. Open your life to receive the increase that is ever available and waiting to be lavished upon you.
14. Have fun.

> You don't have a money problem,
> you have a forgiveness problem.
>
> ·EDWENE GAINES·

Receiving

This is the third side of the abundance square.

"The cost of giving is receiving," *A Course in Miracles* states. Receiving is the most important factor in the abundance equation, one that can be very challenging for many people. I have known exceedingly generous men who are most uncomfortable and awkward when it comes to being on the receiving end of a gift, either a material gift or the gift of a compliment. It is as important to be a gracious receiver as it is to be a generous giver.

At some time you may have had the experience of carefully selecting what you thought was the perfect gift for a friend, wrapping it beautifully and presenting it proudly, only to find your friend's reaction awkward and ungracious. Perhaps your friend even brushed off your gesture with comments like, "It looks too expensive," or "You shouldn't have," or "I already have one very similar," or "I really can't use this." How has such a response caused you to feel? Rejected? Unappreciated? No matter how much effort you put forth, there's no pleasing your friend.

Many of us feel awkward being on the receiving end because we are not in control and view being the receiver as being vulnerable or weak. We feel undeserving, so in our discomfort we brush off another person's act of generosity.

Just as we have to practice giving, so too we have to practice receiving. We must open our minds and hearts to be unrestricted

> The whole world is you.
> Yet you keep thinking there is something else . . .
>
> ·HSUEH-FENG·

conduits through which the energy of giving and receiving may flow freely.

You can begin your practice of receiving by saying "Yes."

"Yes, thank you for picking up the check."

"Yes, thank you for noticing my suit. I'm quite fond of it also."

Be gracious. Develop an accepting, gracious spirit. Learn to say "Yes" to life. Never begrudge people their good. Whenever you feel cheated because you think another person has some good that you desire, stop yourself and realize you have slipped into lack thinking. Celebrate everyone's success, and you'll be opening the byways of your consciousness to receive similar blessings.

For years I've had a tape by that outrageous and flamboyant teacher of prosperity, Reverend Ike. Over and over Reverend Ike exclaims, "That's for me!" Whenever he sees displayed in a swanky shop window a suit of clothing that he wishes he could buy but for which he doesn't have the funds, he declares, "That's for me!" He observes others achieving a level of success he desires, and he shouts, "That's for me!"

Reverend Ike grew up in the ghetto, but he refused to remain in ghetto consciousness. He had higher aspirations. Why, he even wanted to drive a Rolls-Royce, a big, shiny, brown Rolls-Royce, and he would visualize himself in one. As he walked past a Rolls showroom in New York one day, there in the window was a cocoa-brown Rolls-Royce. Ike was so excited that he shouted out loud, "That's for me!"

Time passed, and Reverend Ike practiced living the Prosperity Principle. He eventually became a successful and famous minister who inspired thousands to rise out of the limitation of poverty consciousness and realize they were children of a wealthy Father and heirs to His Kingdom. Reverend Ike got his tailored suits and his dream car as well.

As we practice the Spiritual Law of Abundance, we can and will get things—beautiful, wonderful, exciting things. They can be enjoyable, pleasurable, and rewarding, but we must always remember that they are only things, not who we are, not a measure of our worth.

Having all the money we desire certainly makes living on this planet easier. As Mike Todd once said, "I've been rich and I've been poor. Rich is better." But money, whether we have it or not, is in no way an estimate of our worth. Our worth is invaluable and has been established by God.

God doesn't care if you drive a Yugo or a Rolls-Royce. The question is: Do *you* care? You can have whatever you believe you deserve. You can live in a shanty or on an estate. It is done unto you according to your consciousness.

You must feel deserving in order to receive. You must see yourself as worthy. The following affirmations can help you develop a receiving consciousness.

I, ___________, deserve to receive.

I, ___________, find great pleasure in receiving.

I, ___________, am a gracious receiver.

I, ___________, delight in supporting others in being gracious receivers.

I, ____________, deserve to receive a raise [or love, or a bonus, or a new position, or a great vacation, or . . .].

I, ____________, say yes to life, and life gives back to me a fabulous increase.

Accepting

This side completes the abundance square.

God offers each of us everything. Many people spend a lifetime denying this, through thoughts, through conversations, through actions and non-actions. They deny themselves, and they deny God pleasure by declining God's gifts within their hearts.

To receive a gift, you must accept it.

One of my favorite movies is *Chariots of Fire*. As you may recall, the story is about several young men from diverse backgrounds who are in training to represent Britain on its 1924 Olympic track team. The runners range from a young nobleman, to wealthy Oxford students, to a humble Scottish lad with a dream to become a missionary, but only after he captures the Olympic gold. Eric Liddell was his name, and he was a great inspiration. Eric was from a very religious family, and it was assumed without question that he would serve as a Christian missionary in China. He agreed to this, but first he had to run, and run he did, faster than his competition. Eric ran without proper athletic shoes, without a trainer, without a proper track, and without a support team. He simply ran, and he knew it was his gift from God. His well-meaning sister, concerned that he was devoting more time to running than to his Bible study, spoke to him about his priorities. He gave her the greatest spiritual response I have heard as far as living one's dream:

> Where one door shuts, another opens.
>
> ·SPANISH PROVERB·

 "God . . . God made me fast, and when I run I can feel God's  pleasure."

When we acknowledge the unique gifts from God that are ours and bring them to life, it *is* pleasing to God. The gift is given. The blessing is given. We have received it, but not necessarily accepted it.

This lesson was illustrated to me, more clearly than I could have imagined, with Willie, a counselee of mine on and off for several years. He was an extremely dispirited young man, out of step with most of the world. He regularly saw a psychiatrist, who prescribed antidepressants in an attempt to balance his frequently plummeting mental state. Willie had been severely and permanently traumatized in childhood by his mentally disturbed parents. He would tell me tales of horror about his father that were beyond my ability to grasp. I would do my best to soothe his troubled soul and would pray for his release from his mental anguish. Later I would reflect on what Willie had told me and think, Surely in his present misery he is recalling the past as more horrendous than it actually was. One day he arrived at my office unannounced and begged me to go with him to his father's house. "Maybe if you see how he lives you'll get an idea of what my childhood was like." Willie assured me that his father was out of town and it was safe for us to go.

I knew Willie was from a family of some means, because he had always attended boarding schools, but nothing he had told me could have prepared me for what I saw. His father lived on a large estate. As we drove down the driveway, I could see that the property, with its massive trees and overgrown shrubbery, had not been tended to in years. We got out of the car, and there before us was an enormous house in a state of ruin. It was a scene out of a B-grade horror movie.

I told Willie it wasn't really necessary to go inside; I had a much clearer picture now. What if we just hopped back in the car and left. Willie would hear nothing of it. He had gotten me this far, and he insisted I go inside. Seeing how his father lived, he said, would speak volumes about what and where he had come from, what he had spent years processing. We entered through a back door that led into the kitchen. Before crossing the threshold, the odor, or I should say stench, accosted my nostrils.

Willie's father lived in the kitchen. I do mean *lived* in the kitchen, and only the kitchen. It was piled high with debris and filth. There was a cot, a hotplate, garbage cans overflowing with empty cans and mounds of debris.

"Okay, Willie, I see and smell how your father lives," I said. "Can we please go now?"

"No," Willie stated emphatically. "Just walk through the rest of the house, you have to see the rest." We made our way out of the kitchen, and what I saw next was nearly as startling: room after room of elegant antiques, rich tapestries, and fine art covered in inches of dust. It looked as if the family had walked out of these rooms twenty-five or thirty years before and no one had entered since. Willie then led me upstairs, saying that what he was about to show me was the most important insight into his family history. Upstairs were the bedrooms, and in each room were scores of neatly stacked unopened presents. Gifts of various sizes, all wrapped with fancy but faded paper and bows—pile upon pile of Christmas and birthday presents and other gifts, on dressers, bureaus, chairs, beds, nightstands, chests, and desks.

"Willie," I exclaimed, "what are these?"

"They are the hundreds of gifts my father got from his parents, from my mother before their divorce [which was twenty years earlier], from my aunts, uncles, cousins, and me. He has never, as far back as I can remember, opened any gift given to him."

That's when I learned we can be given gifts, even receive them, without *accepting* them. I also learned that Willie did not exaggerate about his family and how his father chose to live. You and I, like Willie's father, have free will. God gives us every good gift. "It is the Father's good pleasure to give you the Kingdom," but we have to accept the gifts that are given to us. Willie's father chose not to accept his home, his parents, his son's love, his education, or his wealth.

So often we too choose not to accept all that is given to us. We say, "So what do I have that is so unique, so wonderful, so beneficial?" The gifts of God—that's what you have. But these countless and wondrous gifts have no reality for you until you accept them.

Many of us can live our lives like Willie's father, though perhaps more subtly. We have been given gift upon gift, blessing upon blessing, but rather than manifest these divine blessings and unique talents, we hide them away in some dark and dusty recesses of our minds. Then we cry out about how unfair life is and how everyone else seems to have an easier go than we do.

A couple of winters ago I was preparing a Sunday talk on counting our blessings. My consciousness was still full of the material for my lesson when David and I went to a mall to do some errands. Unexpectedly it began to snow, and I started to complain about the snow, how I had new flats on, which were getting wet and were going to get stained, how my feet were cold. I was carrying on as if some tragedy had befallen me.

We entered the mall, and I was still kvetching when I noticed a lone man sitting on a ledge. I looked at him and saw that he had no left leg. It must have been obvious to him that I was staring at him, noticing his disability. The human tendency is to look away quickly, to act as if we hadn't noticed. I try not to do that, so I looked right into his eyes and smiled. He didn't smile back. The man didn't have a leg, and I was complaining about cold feet and stained shoes. "Okay, God, I get it!"

We can act as if a minor inconvenience is a big deal. All of us—including the man at the mall—have been given our unique gifts, and we often take our gifts for granted, or even hide them. We pretend to be little instead of magnificent. It is not arrogant to live as God created us. It is not arrogant to make full use of the gifts He has given us. The Bible tells us that we have been gloriously and wondrously made; but what we do with the glory and wonder contained within is up to us. What we make of ourselves is up to each one of us. This is where we join God as *co-creators*.

Two women I know, Chris and Mary, each have a disability; both have had to learn to live with the ravages of polio, Mary unable to use her legs and Chris able to walk only with braces and crutches. But they don't see themselves as handicapped; rather, they see themselves as ballerinas. Each has made a choice to see herself as unlimited, graceful, feminine, and artistic. Chris and Mary are principal dancers in an extension of the Cleveland Ballet called Dancing Wheels, a wheelchair troupe. The graceful beauty of their performances rushes right into the heart as they share their unique gifts from God fully with their audiences.

Consider what gifts have been given to you that you have denied, turned your attention from, hidden, or left unopened. The next time you're about to send out invitations to your "pity party," count your limitless gifts. You have a mind that can co-create with God. You have the ability to choose what to focus on. You have the ability to direct your thoughts with clear intention.

Ask yourself: Am I truly

without talent?

without a mind?

without abilities?

without power?

without hope?

without faith?

without instinct?

without passion?

without pleasure?

without love?

Am I truly without all these gifts?

The spiritual truth for each of us as God's children is that we are remarkably blessed. We must open our eyes, hearts, and consciousness fully, and recognize that this is so.

Matthew Fox, in his book *Original Blessing*, says that "beauty has to do with seeing all of life as a blessing." When we discover our gifts, open them, use them, we practice being good receivers of the beauty of life. We shift from the negative "Woe is me" to "I am one of the most blessed people on the planet."

We are all incredibly blessed, and you *are* one of the most blessed. Your blessings and gifts can increase only by your accepting them. Begin to live as a blessed one. Give to others the extension of the blessings you have received. Look upon others with the love you have now been willing to accept. *You carry the imprint of God within you.* That divine pattern is written within your heart and upon your soul. It is the truth of your being; it is a Spiritual Principle from which you can choose to live your life.

> *Concerning spiritual gifts, I do not want you to be uninformed. . . . There are a variety of gifts, but the same Spirit, and there are a variety of services, but the same Lord. And there are a variety of abilities, but the same God gives abilities to everyone for their service. The Spirit's presence is shown in some way in each one, for the good of all.*
>
> I CORINTHIANS 12:1–7

We all have been given a number of spiritual gifts. Paul elaborates on some, listing wisdom, knowledge, faith, ability to heal, to be a miracle worker, to speak for God, to discern the messages of truth from the message of the ego. It is up to us, individually, to discover and accept our unique gifts. It is our responsibility to use these gifts of God, not just for our own betterment, but also to help the advancement of others.

Your unique gifts may be extended to bless your family, your friends, your students, your colleagues. Some people find their circle of influence widening as they make a positive difference in more and more lives. Individuals who have been touched by your unique goodness in turn extend what they have received from you, and the energy of positive influence continues to flow.

Among the spiritual gifts we may extend to others are true love, the ability to be a loving person to all; the ability to bring joy out in other people; honesty, the ability to be true to ourselves and be who we are no matter where we are or whom we are with.

Knowing our unique spiritual gift is a blessing in itself, and it will lead doors to open for us, so that we may enter rooms where we can express our uniqueness fully and freely.

Years ago I realized that my unique spiritual gift is the ability to see the divine in everyone. Without difficulty, I am able to see the divine, the Christ-Spirit in others. At a deep level of being, this gift always abided in me, but I was not always conscious of having it. It came full-bloom into my consciousness at a time of spiritual awakening for me. It has never diminished and it has never expanded, because it didn't have to. It was complete. I am ever thankful for this gift, for it allows me to be with a person who is gravely ill or dying, or with one who is excelling or depressed or jumping through hoops, and I can see the same God-Spirit in all of them. I can see each as a divine self. As I matured with this wonderful gift, it has become an asset in my expanding work as a minister; in recent years it has gently guided me into my broader work as author and lecturer.

You too have some unique spiritual gifts. You also have the means to discover what they are and to learn from them. Once you recognize what your gift or gifts are, you must use them. Just as any skill, such as playing the piano or dancing or programming computers, requires steadfast practice in order to achieve mastery, you must practice using your gifts. You have to apply them consciously and consistently. Only then can they become yours, and become second nature. You need to remember to use these gifts of God in all situations and with all people.

You don't need to decide whether you're worthy of such gifts;

that decision has already been made. It was made by God when He placed His Spirit in you, and that same spirit is leading you to discover your unique gifts, to accept them, and to create a life of beauty, fulfillment, and abundance out of them.

Here are some affirmations to help you realize your unique spiritual gifts:

I, ___________, am deserving of the best God has to offer.

I, ___________, delight in accepting and living out of my unique gifts of God.

I, ___________, now attract and accept infinite possibilities for good into my life.

I, ___________, am unique.

I, ___________, have unique talents to share with the world.

There is a spot for me, and me alone, to fill in life.

I, ___________, am willing to discover my unique talents.

The more I, ___________, live out of my unique talents, the more joy and success I experience.

To live the abundant life, we must faithfully practice all four aspects of our square—blessing, giving, receiving, and accepting. As you continue to develop your spiritual muscles through your consistent application of the Spiritual Law of Abundance, your life blessings and wonders and good will flow to you in greater measure than you have ever imagined. It isn't magic, but it is miraculous.

Free at Last

The Spiritual Law of Forgiveness

11

An old Johnny Mercer–Harold Arlen song tells us to "accentuate the positive, eliminate the negative, latch on to the affirmative, don't mess with Mr. In-Between." It has a peppy melody and carries a wise and simple message.

"Eliminate the negative" is a great spiritual message. It sounds so easy when sung to a cheery melody, but few of us find it an easy or cheery process. First, we must be aware of exactly what in our lives is negative, nonsupportive, and toxic. Next, we must honestly examine our inner thoughts around these negatives and look at what purpose they may have served. Many of us, for example, stay in unhealthy, dysfunctional relationships because we feel incapable of supporting ourselves. We live with this unhealthy decision because either we feel it's the best we could do or it allows us to be dependent and avoid emotional responsibility for our own lives. We have to look long and hard at ourselves and decide whether we truly desire our future to be

> The wise boldly pick up a truth as soon as they hear it.
> Don't wait for a moment, or you'll lose your head.
>
> ·HSUEH-DOU·

different from our past. If the answer is yes, we can begin to work with the freeing Law of Forgiveness.

"Forgiveness offers everything I want," *A Course in Miracles* says. Forgiveness is the way we cleanse our minds. As we successfully work with forgiveness, we clear away the old, worn-out, stagnant energy that blocks our growth. We leave space into which we can invite new, supportive, life-affirming energy, circumstances, and people to enter our lives. We take a stand for what we do want, rather than battle with what we say we don't want. The more we engage in the activity of forgiveness, the more we can see what else needs to be released through ongoing forgiveness.

One of the most helpful ways to practice the freeing quality of letting go, which is the end result of forgiveness, is to clean out the clutter in our lives. We often accumulate so much junk and don't know what to do with it. We stuff it in a folder, cram it in a drawer, shove it in the back of a closet. If we do this enough we create a mess—in our homes, offices, and cars, and in our souls as well.

When we clean out such messes we open our consciousness and our lives to order and ease. Some people get a kick out of getting money for their discarded treasures, by selling them to secondhand stores or holding a garage sale. I'm satisfied simply to give things away with no strings attached. However you clean out your physical environment and let go of the material things, you allow openness and abundance to enter your life. Practice daily eliminating whatever you have that no longer serves you or brings you joy. Likewise practice eliminating the clutter of thoughts, not only old grievances that do not serve you, but also recent thinking that gets in the way of forgiveness.

Here's the story of a woman who faced the challenge of letting go. Felicity and Scott had been married six years when she discovered he had been having an intermittent affair with a colleague for the previous eighteen months. She was heartsick and wanted nothing more to do with him, and asked him to leave their home. Felicity did not want a divorce for several reasons. She knew their daughters, ages two and four, adored their daddy and he them. Divorce was also very much against her religious upbringing. Her parents, although supportive of her decision to marry Scott, were never entirely convinced he was right for her, and not hesitant in letting her know. If she mentioned her problems to them, she knew, they would be quick to say, "We told you so."

If she sought and obtained an annulment, it would mean declaring the marriage never really happened. That was unthinkable to Felicity. She felt betrayed, abandoned, defiled, and alone; not even her religion was offering her solace. Felicity had always been interested in personal growth and self-improvement and was familiar with some teachings on forgiveness. In her head she "knew" she had to forgive Scott, but her heart wasn't as sure.

While she was trying to force herself to forgive Scott, he was begging her to forgive him and take him back. He loved her, he was sorry, and he would never do that to her or their family or himself again. Scott was relentless in his pursuit of Felicity and his desire to return home. After several weeks of his promises, she took him back into their home, but not their bed. She just couldn't, she told him.

While she was attempting to forgive Scott, she was constantly wrestling with the image of him with the other woman. After a few weeks Scott returned to the bedroom, but Felicity found herself faking pleasure when she was intimate with Scott. Outside the bedroom she was more and more demanding, and she insisted on knowing his whereabouts every moment. She checked on him constantly and always felt he owed her, and no matter what he did it could never be enough to soothe the pain he had caused her. Felicity was becoming a bitter woman, believing all men were cheats and liars, not to be trusted.

She would work on forgiving him, but she would never forget what he had done to her and their family. This lukewarm attempt at forgiveness, the forgive-but-never-forget variety, is really not forgiveness. It is what *A Course in Miracles* calls "false forgiveness," which is actually an attack, not forgiveness:

> False forgiveness continues to keep in the foreground what awful deed was done.
>
> False forgiveness means we see ourselves as victims and others as perpetrators.
>
> False forgiveness means we withhold love and the possibility of healing.
>
> False forgiveness means we really damn and then attempt to "make nice."
>
> False forgiveness means we see others as evil rather than as people just like us who have made mistakes.
>
> False forgiveness is based on fear and clings to guilt.
>
> False forgiveness is a withholding of love.
>
> False forgiveness is attack.

> You cannot avoid paradise.
> You can only avoid seeing it.
>
> ·CHARLOTTE JOKO BECK·

While living in a state of false forgiveness, Felicity and Scott would never be able to heal their relationship, a relationship consisting of one wounded victim and one guilty enemy. It could not work and was doomed to misery. We must give Felicity credit, though, for she was doing the best she could, and dealing with limited emotional resources.

Her forgiveness was more of a "should" than a spiritual practice. Out of guilt and shame she allowed Scott back into their home and bed long before she was mentally, emotionally, and physically ready. She was subconsciously always trying to make Scott pay for what he had done to her, always reminding him and attempting to keep his feelings of guilt very much alive. Love cannot grow in such an environment. What Scott and Felicity did nine months later was what they needed to do initially: they went into counseling as a couple and individually.

In counseling Scott explored what was underlying his need to seek sexual intimacy outside the marriage. Remember "I am never upset for the reason I think"? Well, they both worked with that; they connected with the anger and rage that had been buried within them and learned to discharge it in appropriate ways. Then they both worked on true forgiveness of self and the other. It never occurred to Felicity that she needed to forgive herself, but buried in her were many harsh and critical thoughts about her value and worth and worthiness. As she forgave herself she opened her heart to love herself; then she could begin to work on forgiving Scott, not from a position of denying her pain, not from a sense of "should," but from a willingness to be whole and free. Forgiveness is the price we pay for our own freedom.

Felicity began to practice true forgiveness:

True forgiveness is healing.

True forgiveness is restoring our minds to purity and innocence.

True forgiveness is for all.

True forgiveness takes away all barriers that have stood between us and another.

True forgiveness heals all involved.

True forgiveness heals our fear-filled nightmares.

True forgiveness is our collective function.

True forgiveness is letting go of guilt.

True forgiveness looks beyond our error.

True forgiveness brings heaven closer to our awareness.

True forgiveness offers miracles to everyone.

True forgiveness offers everything we want.

True forgiveness brings us fully into the present.

Forgiveness allows us to reinterpret what has occurred from a much more enlightened state of mind. Our perceptions are purified and not only can we see the situation more clearly, we can see through the situation to the truth that lies beyond. We can see why something occurred in order to support us in waking up or becoming empowered or facing a deep fear.

A recurring theme in my teaching is the necessity to forgive, and to forgive until we no longer feel even the slightest pang of pain from the previous hurt. We need to forgive until we have healed every scrap of fear, every painful memory. This does not happen out of a sense of "should," as Felicity discovered. It occurs through repeatedly and fully engaging in forgiveness techniques. There is no set formula, no quick fix, and no getting around the need to forgive if we want to be free of old and present conflict and pain—if we want to be happy!

The 70 × 7 Technique

There is a New Testament story about one of the apostles, who comes to Jesus and poses a question: If someone has done you wrong, offended you in some way, just how many times is he to be forgiven? The apostle then answers his own question by suggesting: Seven times. Jesus responds: Not seven times but seven times seventy. This was truly a new thought, a radically outrageous idea, to keep forgiving a perceived offense until the forgiving individual had completely released it. Seven times seventy doesn't mean 490. It merely symbolizes the need to forgive without counting, and it indicates that forgiveness must be a lifelong, continuous process.

Here is an excellent technique for clearing out the mental and soul clutter that may be clouding your awareness. For one week, write seventy times each day: *I now forgive myself for all known and unknown limitations I have placed upon myself and others.* Writing the affirmation seventy times a day is a lot of writing. Do it in longhand, not on a typewriter or computer.

As you engage in such a high level of committed forgiveness work, you are forgiving yourself and others, freeing everyone from the chains of resentment and smoldering grievances. Your

> A moment's insight is sometimes worth a life's experience.
>
> ·OLIVER WENDELL HOLMES·

forgiveness turns the world from one of hurt, suffering, and judgment into one of light, healing, love, and freedom. Forgiveness transforms your vision and illuminates your mind. Forgiveness restores your mind to peace and offers you miracles.

Some years ago, I had done so much deep forgiveness work that I thought I had done it all and dealt with every fear. But God knew there was a collective fear buried in my consciousness, and my consciousness drew me to six years of dealing with what many people in our country fear more than anything—the IRS!

If you don't harbor a deep-seated fear of the IRS, I'm sure you know people who do. I used to be one of those fearful. Here is what happened: I was audited for several years in a row, the IRS having received a report from someone who told them I was making a huge amount of money and not reporting it. This was laughable. My husband had given up a very successful position in Chicago and moved to Cleveland for us to be married, and in our first years together our combined income had dropped by more than sixty percent. We really had to work, and work we did, on our prosperity consciousness. The IRS sent not one, but two agents to comb through every detail of my life. The charge was groundless and the audit time-consuming, and I was intimidated by the agents. I was distraught. It was costing us thousands of dollars we did not have to retain the top accounting firm that had always done my taxes to represent me.

A few days before an important meeting with accountants

and IRS agents, I called a minister friend, Edwene Gaines, whom I call the "queen of prosperity," to ask for moral support and prayer, and for help in quelling my fear. (You may think, Why fear if you are innocent? The circumstances of an audit themselves are intimidating, and I'd never been in such circumstances. And yet there I was.) Edwene shared with me a funny yet effective affirmation: "The IRS can't eat me." The night before the meeting, I affirmed again and again, "The IRS can't eat me," until I finally drifted off to sleep at about three a.m. In the morning, as the agents asked me question after question, demanding details from the previous decade, I kept silently affirming, "The IRS can't eat me!" There were moments when I doubted this and could almost see their cauldron bubbling!

One agent asked, "Do you have any foreign bank accounts?" "You mean like Swiss?" I asked, astonished. "Yes," the agent replied. I could not contain myself; I burst out laughing while my accountants tried to swallow their smirks. I didn't have an extra twenty dollars, let alone a Swiss bank account. "The IRS can't eat me."

When I was ordained, in 1979, ministers were allowed to opt out of Social Security if they desired. I had never believed the government to be my source—I knew God was—and I had not contributed much in the few years since college. So I opted out and filled out the appropriate form. I never thought about it again until I was under the IRS microscope. The agents requested my copy of the form. I had not been the most organized person as far as files and paperwork. (I have since learned to be more organized, thanks to the IRS.) I began searching for this form, now more than a decade old. I could not find it and my heart sank. I got a bill from the IRS for back Social Security payments due, for $12,000. It might as well have been $12

> The world is a passage back to God, that is the only reason it is here.
>
> · MICHAEL MURPHY ·

million. There was no way I could pay it, and I knew I did not owe it. I filed an extension and kept searching. "The IRS can't eat me."

Nothing short of that one piece of paper was enough proof that it had been filed. The Social Security Administration couldn't help me. It kept its records for only seven years, so it did not have a copy of the form. The responsibility was solely mine. The fact that the IRS had never questioned this each year I had filed taxes made no difference. The fact that the information was even written on an earlier tax return made no difference. My troubles with the IRS went on for years, six as I said. My affirmation went from "The IRS can't eat me" to "God bless the IRS," and I meant it. I don't think too many people pray for the IRS. In my meetings I was dealing with real flesh-and-blood people, and I saw that not only can the IRS not eat me, but also that the IRS is us, real people who work for a government agency that most people fear.

I went to court over this matter, knowing that I was right. And yet I lost—I didn't have that piece of paper. It was a tremendous shock. Each day added interest to the original $12,000, and in the end our monthly payments to the IRS were only slightly less than our mortgage. I had to dig to find the blessing. What I learned was:

1. The IRS can't eat me or any of us.
2. They are not to be feared, they are us. They are people just like us.

3. God is my Source. (New avenues of abundance opened soon after.)
4. It's better to be organized, and to file all important documents safely. An accountant is the best person to handle all important matters.
5. I was empowered by forgiving the IRS and blessing it with each payment.
6. It's only money.

Fear of the IRS is a collective drama many people participate in. I no longer do. I no longer fear the IRS. What we don't forgive, we fear. I got through my experience by writing a lot of forgiveness lists. I wrote some for the IRS and the collective fear, many for the person who had reported me, who was a very hurt person, and many for myself for not being more organized. I learned to see the error in this episode. It wasn't sin, which judges and condemns. Error calls for correction. Correction was made. God has graciously blessed me in countless ways. I was forced to face my fear of the IRS and rise above it. I learned a valuable lesson, and I now have Social Security. I'm not sure I want it, but I have it.

This experience seemed unfair, but the only way to be free of it was to stop trying to prove my innocence, to forgive and let it go. This was very difficult for me, a person who really stands for integrity and the truth prevailing. When I chose freedom of mind over proving to the IRS that I opted out of Social Security, new doors of opportunity and good opened in my life and David's. I thought of Jesus' words: "Render unto Caesar the things that are Caesar's and unto God the things that are God's." I no longer had to prove Spiritual Principle to the IRS. I just had to move on in my life. Letting the problem go was certainly worth the peace of mind that followed. My prayer partner Marleen suggested that I think of the IRS bill as another utility payment, not as some unfair or unjust debt or penalty. That helped me perceive the situation differently.

A key in letting a nagging situation go is to see it differently. To see our problems differently means that we are willing to let them go. Once we let go, an answer, a solution perhaps beyond our normal reasoning, can offer itself to us. While we cling to our problems, this possibility is closed to us. Every problem in our lives is really an error in our thinking brought to our awareness to be resolved, to be healed. We can do something about the problem. Errors can be corrected; they actually call for correction.

I have learned to turn perceived problems over to the Holy Spirit. I give them with a prayer: "Look, I gave this the best that I was able to give, and it's still a problem. I give it to you to use for your purpose." When we give a problem to the Holy Spirit to be solved, we want it to be solved. As long as I struggled with the IRS, I made the accuser's attack on me real. When I released it, I was no longer joining her in her illusion. This was the only way the problem could end.

A Course in Miracles asks, "Is it not possible that all your problems have been solved, but you have removed yourself from the solution?" This is an empowering thought. I often ask people, "What would you talk about if you had no problems to concern yourself with?"

Here is a tricky technique to practice over a weekend. Put an ordinary rubber band around your wrist, and each time you are mentally engaged in negative thinking or are talking or obsessing about a perceived problem, give that rubber band a little snap. Not a bruise-your-wrist snap, but an "Excuse me, please pay attention to how negative you're being" snap. When you feel ready, try it for an entire week. We think we have an up attitude, accentuating the

Luis de Leon, returning to his university after five years' imprisonment by the Inquisition, resumed his lectures with the words: "As we were saying yesterday . . ."

·SPANISH PARABLE·

positive, but just beneath our conscious awareness is a lot of unresolved negativity. This little exercise helps us spot that.

This is release at work. We have the power to say no to the undesired negativity in our lives. We can release negative thoughts, feelings, ideas, and beliefs from collective and individual consciousness. When we engage this power and truly release, we create a vacuum. What is the Universal Principle concerning vacuums? "Nature abhors a vacuum." Nature, life itself, the Universe, is going to see to it that the vacuum gets filled. As we create a vacuum by releasing worn-out states of mind and being, we must fill that vacuum immediately with what we want. It is going to be filled, that we can't prevent, so we may as well do it consciously and get what we desire, rather than allow it to be filled with another dose of negativity.

As we familiarize ourselves with this power of mind we must eliminate the ancient false notion that to be holy in God's eyes we must lead lives of deprivation, stricken with misery and with every conceivable lack. Such limited beliefs result in dysfunction, restriction, toxic emotions, and racial and sexual bondage. Conscious beings no longer seek to renounce their good or physical pleasure; they will renounce old fear, inhibition, and inconsistencies, to cast off physical, mental, and spiritual limitations.

We cannot strive toward perfection until false notions have

been cleansed from our consciousness. We must eliminate from our thought all ideas or attitudes that might interfere with the full expression of our true divine nature. When this expression is a reality, the way is opened for the free flow of Spirit.

Life is a constant spiral of growth, and for this growth to proceed without hindrance, the old good, even that which once served us, must be eliminated to make way for the new, greater good. As Jesus said, you can't put new wine into an old wineskin: you can't put a new idea into an old container. If new wine filled with new life was put into an old wineskin, the old container would deteriorate, rot, and crumble.

Here are two affirmations to help you with releasing:

I, __________, willingly release old, worn-out thoughts, feelings, beliefs, and things that clutter my life and consciousness.

I, __________, purge my mind of dead thoughts and dead relationships: I am free.

As you practice engaging with the principle of elimination, you are consciously rejecting everything in your life that does not conform to Spiritual Principle.

After we have released through forgiveness, it is necessary to tune in to what we want. We must fill the vacuum with the good we desire, or the previous mental occupants, our old habits, will move back in. Keep your focus on what you do want and off what you don't want. Think about what is good and pure, right and holy for you. Fill your mind, heart, and soul with beauty and peace, and live a life forgiven.

Uncoiling the Sleeping Life Force

The Spiritual Law of Divine Life 12

The Spiritual Reality of our being is that we arrived complete. If we visit a hospital nursery and look at the newborns there, we are struck by their perfection and precious beauty, their innocence and purity, their softness and vulnerability, and yet their aliveness and wholeness.

We all come into this world unsullied, beautiful, innocent, and fully alive, and with every blessing. As we mature, these innate gifts are either recognized and nurtured or go unacknowledged, maybe even belittled and stifled. As children we quickly learn to seek our validation in our immediate surroundings, and unless our wonder and wholeness are nourished and celebrated, our innate sense of completion erodes and eventually goes into hiding.

We are born perfect children of God, and our families either recognize this or do not. Our arrival is celebrated or is not. As children we are either seen or unseen.

> The journey is the reward.
>
> ·CHINESE SAYING·

Before a seen child is born, there is much excitement and anticipation. After birth, the child is honored, loved, cuddled, and adored by family and friends. The unseen child, in contrast, does not receive such a welcoming celebration and is ignored most of the time—from conception through birth and throughout the years of growing up.

Whether one is a seen or an unseen child has nothing to do with economics, education, or social standing. It has everything to do with how healed the parents are and how seen they are themselves.

Seen children mature with their innate sense of self-worth intact. Although they have much to learn and experience on a social level, they are always grounded in the inner level of spirit, always attuned to the inner life force. While people can rise from an unseen upbringing and become fully seen adults, it requires enormous commitment, as is illustrated in the stories of several individuals in this book.

My husband was born and brought up a seen child. David's parents were overjoyed with their beautiful baby boy. They kept a journal of his growth, activities, and antics, writing in it several times a week from his birth to age six. They loved him and did everything they could to nurture his curiosity, intelligence, athletic abilities, and spirit. The emerging life force in him was celebrated. As a result he matured with a deep sense of inner confidence and self-reliance.

Seeing Yourself

If you realize you were born as an unseen child, you can begin to return to your innate wholeness by celebrating your life:

1. Every morning, stand in front of the mirror naked and love the person before you. Love all her body parts, whether or not you approve of their size and shape. Praise her unseen aspects, acknowledging her soul and goodness. Say loving, kind, encouraging things.
2. Keep a photograph of yourself as a child of three or four with you. If you don't have a photo of yourself at that age, draw a picture. Then look at that tiny person you once were, someone who still lives within you, and love that child now in a way he or she was perhaps never loved. Tell the child how good, precious, and uniquely talented he or she is.
3. Ask that young, inner child what he or she would like to do. Take the child out to play, go on a picnic, climb rocks, visit an amusement park or the zoo, make mud pies, play pirates. Buy the child a toy. Show the child you are. Indulge your inner child. Have fun! Nurture the life force!

As you pursue these activities with your inner child, he or she will begin to leave the shell that has been home for so many years to enter a world of play and joy and celebration.

I too was born and raised as a seen child, and I continue to be my parents' much-loved daughter. But being seen and spiritually connected does not mean being immune from pain and crisis, as the story below demonstrates. It does, however, mean we may have tools and understand how to use them.

I listened to the doctor's voice on the phone, and my whole being reeled in stunned horror. "Cancer! Cancer! Cancer!" my head began to scream. No, this could not be, not me, a daily meditator for two decades. This could not be happening to me, me who was always working on my inner self, me who had never smoked a cigarette or led a wild life. This could not be happening to me, who hadn't eaten meat in twenty years, and drank only purified water. Not me, who had always cared for my spirit, soul, and body. Not me, the minister, who was always tending to the spiritual needs and physical crises of others.

Unaware of the impact of her words, the doctor continued. I momentarily entered her reality. "You'll have to repeat yourself," I said. "I'm not focusing." After that most awful life-robbing one, *cancer*, I was unable to hear another word. I was numb, and my ears were ringing. "I can't hear you," I managed to choke out. On she talked: ". . . Surgery immediately, a hysterectomy . . . stages . . . survival rates." "Oh my God," I thought, "I'm going to die, and I've just begun to truly live." My mind raced on.

I received the diagnosis of uterine cancer over the phone. As a woman minister for more than a dozen years, I had spent time with many people facing this dreadful disease, but not until I heard the words spoken about me did the terror strike me. I learned how to face those feelings, move through them, and take charge of my own destiny. I learned all this in light of a life-challenging crisis. After hearing the diagnosis of cancer I deeply questioned and examined every belief and teaching I had embraced for the previous twenty years.

Sometimes in spiritual, metaphysical teachings there can be a tendency to oversimplify and find a quick, easy, and pat answer.

> I should never have made my success in life if I had not bestowed upon the least thing I have ever undertaken the same attention and care I have bestowed upon the greatest.
>
> ·CHARLES DICKENS·

Having an illness can be viewed as a failure in demonstrating the workings of the Law. There is then not only the terror of the disease, but guilt over having the disease as well. I am reminded of the simple thought from the Buddhist teacher. "Is this [idea] helpful?" Obviously it is not. It is not helpful at all.

In my state of absolute horror at the diagnosis, I called a friend of mine, Peter, who is an advanced disciple of Bhakti, the yoga of spiritual devotion, and had lived many years in India. I told him the information and shared my conflicted emotions about how I, a spiritual teacher, a vegetarian, a teacher of love and forgiveness, could have cancer. He calmly replied, "Many of the greatest saints in India died of cancer, and that did not diminish their teachings or holiness."

"Yes," I responded, "but I'm a metaphysician, and metaphysics views all outer experiences as reflections of an inner state of mind, so if my mind had buried thoughts of cancer I wasn't aware of them on any level." Peter said the same words: "Joan, many of the greatest saints in India died of cancer, and that did not diminish their teachings or holiness." I calmed down enough to hear him, as he went on: "This experience that you will go through is not for you alone, because through it you will teach many others."

I knew that fearful, angry, or hurt states of mind can weaken our immune systems. Decades before this diagnosis all of those states were in my consciousness. I also knew that from age thirteen or so I had had considerable female discomfort and problems, including two miscarriages by age twenty-three. Perhaps I was deeply hurt by that, and by the fact that I was unable to have children. The process of looking for a corresponding state of mind to connect with various illnesses can give some insight, but obviously that insight is limited. We can have a genetic predisposition for a particular disorder, or it could be the result of living near a toxic site or of ingesting toxic products. All of this will have a negative impact on our health.

What I gleaned from my experiences were many blessings, and I will share some of the most significant:

- I had thought I was invincible. Now I came to treasure the very fact of being alive.
- I had been giving myself away to such an extent that there was no "me" left for myself. I stopped giving so much of myself away.
- I learned to say no and not feel guilty—okay, I still feel slightly guilty.
- I dramatically changed how I worked.
- I started taking a month off every year to recharge my batteries.
- I started taking two days off in a row, something I had not done in years.
- I began meditating two hours every day.
- I cleared out everything in my life that was attached to littleness and was draining.

- I began doing for myself rather than only and always for others.
- I wrote *A Course in Love.*
- I learned to stop storing up my turmoil, and learned to express myself when I felt upset.
- I lightened up—I stopped placing so much importance on the inconsequential, which had so often been my focus.

Through my experience I became increasingly empowered. I was fully engaged in my healing process, and with the operation and other medical procedures. I recalled the words of Bernie Siegel, which when I first read them I had no idea would someday apply to me: "Those who survive cancer are those who stay in charge. They are the 'difficult patients' because they question everything and know what is going on with their bodies. They are totally involved, knowledgeable, and informed."

So many people just take their diseased bodies and turn them over to the medical profession, abdicating any responsibility or involvement. "Here's my sick body, see what you can do with it," they seem to say. This attitude does not support total healing.

As I was well aware of the connection of spirit, mind, and body, I wanted to have a cassette tape playing through headphones for me during the surgery. David and I would record affirmations, with music in the background. I told the admissions clerk about the tape and my intentions. She would have to okay it with the surgeon, she said. "Oh no," David and I replied in unison. I told her, "I'm not asking permission. This is my body, my mind, my soul, and my life. The tape will calm me and remind me to stay connected with my Source." She immediately agreed and obviously didn't feel the need to check with anyone else.

In cases of illness, whether of mind or body, we can go apart and become centered in prayer and meditation, and consciously tune in to Divine Life with our earnest desire, and call upon the life force centered at the base of the spine to awaken. As this sleeping giant is activated, the perfection of life, which is already present, is called forth. If we experience illness, we have attracted it into our experience, not because we have missed the mark, but for our soul's growth, for spiritual attainment, for mastery, for the power of God to be made manifest through us and this experience.

Divine Life

If you are ever faced with illness, still yourself in Divine Life, call that Divine Life to come forward and radiate through the condition to heal and transform everything now. You might activate this power by playing soft, peaceful music. Go into a meditative state, speak gently and lovingly to your body, instructing it to relax, and when you are feeling calm, declare, first silently, then aloud, over and over:

Life, Life, Life.

Mentally travel through the various parts and functions of your body. As you practice this, you will feel a surge of life well up within you. Consciously send this energy into the area of your affliction. If the affliction is a general lack of vitality, direct the energy up your spinal column. You are thereby tapping into the life force and releasing it into the vital organs and functions of the body.

If you feel depressed, lethargic, bored, discouraged, run-

> It takes a long time to become young.
>
> ·PABLO PICASSO·

down, exhausted, out of sorts, it is time to call forth the power of Life. Affirm "Life, Life, Life" until you feel the life force surge through you and resume its flow. 

When the life force is diminished in us or out of balance, we tend to be controlled by our worldly appetites, always wanting more and more—whether it be food, sex, material goods, approval, love, acknowledgment, power. We individually must control these appetites, rather than have them control us.

I am reminded here of Georgia, a dear friend of mine. The goodness of her heart was vast, a rare treasure. She had lived and traveled around the world, and had spun herself a global web of friends, friends who were closer than family. Georgia's family never understood her: she was different from them, she never did what was expected of her. She had heard the beat of a different drummer early in life, and had followed it.

Georgia joined the Peace Corps after graduate school and spent several years working in orphanages in India and Nepal. She loved the children she cared for; two of them crawled into her heart forever, an Indian boy and a Nepalese girl. It took years of wading through bureaucratic red tape to complete the foreign adoptions; but Georgia knew these were "her children," and nothing would stop her. With her enormous heart, she accepted all people just the way they were—except herself. She never judged or criticized another person—except herself. She was forever willing to do whatever was needed for anyone, friend, neighbor, stranger, it didn't matter—except herself.

> Let life happen to you. Believe me:
> Life is in the right, always.
>
> ·RAINER MARIA RILKE·

On her last trip to Asia Georgia became ill and spent several weeks in agony at a friend's apartment. She was unwilling to go to a doctor, believing the condition would pass. She returned to the States when she was able, still extremely sick and in great pain. She insisted it was fatigue, nothing more. Finally, unable to work and carry on her import business, and still refusing medical assistance, Georgia consented to see a Chinese herbalist. Her health continued to decline over the next several months, until her pain was so severe that a concerned friend persuaded her to go to the hospital.

By then, after months of ignoring the messages her body was sending her, it was too late. She had an aggressive strain of cancer that had spread into several vital organs. None of the doctors offered her any hope. Georgia regretted the delay in seeking medical help; now that she had, it was, sadly, too late. This warm soul departed too soon, leaving hundreds of people around the world in mourning, asking, Why? Why had this intelligent woman refused to take care of her body and its needs, why had she refused to listen to its messages?

Perhaps on a soul level she knew she was complete. Perhaps she was tired and wanted out of the long struggle for acceptance from her family. Whatever her reasons may have been, only she will know. Perhaps those of us she left behind have learned the value of listening to the body, being attuned to its calls of distress not after the signals have been flashing for a year or two, but right away. The body does speak to us, and we must listen and respond while there is still time.

One evening more than a century ago, a middle-class midwestern couple named Charles and Myrtle Fillmore went to a lecture, at Myrtle's prompting. This night would change their lives, and much later millions of other lives.

Myrtle and Charles walked into the lecture hall seeking even the slightest ray of hope. The mother of three young boys, Myrtle suffered from severe tuberculosis, a condition she believed she had inherited from female relatives who had all succumbed to the disease. Myrtle's prospects were grim: life in a sanitorium separated from her family, and an early death. This was unacceptable to the couple, and they were diligently following any promise of hope. A turning point came this evening in 1889, when the couple attended their first metaphysical lecture, presented by a Professor Weeks. In his inspiring presentation Weeks delivered a message that resonated in Myrtle's soul and stirred the sleeping life force within her. "You are a child of God and therefore cannot inherit illness."

That night Myrtle grasped this transformative idea. "You are a child of God and therefore cannot inherit illness." The slumbering life force within her began to stir. She opened herself to the possibility of healing, and her weakened body regained strength and vitality. For years Myrtle had experienced the mental drain of poor physical health. Through affirmative prayer and meditation, the very thought of illness was healed, and replaced with thoughts of life, health, and vitality. Myrtle's mind was rid of thoughts of disease, and the result was a healed body.

Myrtle, once given the prognosis of early death, went on to

> Since everything is but an apparition
> Perfect in being what it is,
> Having nothing to do with good or bad,
> Acceptance or rejection,
> One may as well burst out in laughter.
>
> ·LONGCHENPA·

live for fifty more years. She replaced old, ego-based thoughts with new, spiritually true thoughts. She accepted her wholeness in God and was healed. Her case demonstrates what can and does happen when people awaken and fully engage the "coiled serpent" of the life force. The life force is coiled like a powerful serpent at the first chakra, one of the seven centers of energy located along the spinal column. This energy, known by the Sanskrit word *kundalini*, and also called the "holy stream of life," will rise freely when it is time.

There can be a spontaneous awakening and surge through the spinal cord and chakras, as happened for me nearly twenty years ago while I was in very deep meditation. My body began to pulsate from the root chakra gradually ascending upward, until this vibrating force reached my head and then moved out in great streams of light. As this energy passed through each of the seven chakras, I felt it swirling and expanding. It was an enlivening, awakening experience that opened not only the wheels of energy, but also my entire consciousness, to what William James referred to as those "other realities." The flimsiest of screens had been parted, and I glimpsed at what lies beyond our three-dimensional world.

You may or may not have had your own similar experiences. Such experiences should never be coerced. The life force within you will awaken at the appropriate time. Do not be fearful of it. Relax into the experience as you tap into the wellspring of wonder within you, which awaits your invitation to awaken and rise into your wholeness, and realize what is possible for you.

People often seem to sleepwalk through life. This need not be. For we each carry locked within us the very life of God. I think of the words by Christopher Fry in his poem "The Sleep of Prisoners": "It takes so many thousand years to wake / But will you wake for pity's sake."

Commit now to awaken and live life as a higher-order being. Awaken to your potential. Awaken to your good. Awaken to your spiritual self. Awaken!

> The Zen "genius" sleeps in every one of us and demands an awakening.
>
> ·D. T. SUZUKI·

Putting It All Together

13

You need not read the chapters of *A Course in Life* sequentially. It is not necessary for you to engage fully the Spiritual Law of Faith in chapter 1, for example, in order to start discovering and living your Divine Purpose as taught in chapter 2. Yet all twelve of the spiritual building blocks to a fulfilling and happy life need to work in harmony together. Some will be easy for you, as they may be ways of thinking and living that you already practice. Others may take years to develop and understand completely.

We cannot isolate, separate, or divide these Spiritual Laws and expect them to sustain us, any more than we could separate our hand from our arm and expect to lift a paintbrush. Each law must be engaged, given importance, remembered, and integrated with the others. Our Faith needs to be grounded in Wisdom, our Joy balanced with Non-Attachment, our Love coupled with Power. Our Divine Purpose leads us to reap all the Abundance we could desire. Forgiveness and Love expand our capacity to receive the blessings of the Spiritual Laws.

This journey of the soul is not a linear undertaking, but rather a never-ending spiral that ever expands into the Universal level and expands deep into the soul level. *A Course in Life* is about fully engaging our encoded spirituality, no longer giving it lip service or diminished attention. Remember, complexity is of the ego and simplicity is of the Spirit. This course is simple and will be easy for you if you are willing for it to be so. You already have the power to change anything that you don't want and to attract everything that you do want.

As your familiarity with Universal Laws increases, you will see them at work in a variety of life's expressions, from a theatrical production, to Native American ritual, to your own transcendental experience alone with the beauty of nature. The more you rely on these Laws to work for you, the more you will experience their perfection and see the Universal perfection in your life. A transformative episode in my own life engaged all twelve of the Universal Laws.

Early one cold December morning I was keeping company with Dr. Wayne Dyer, the popular best-selling author of *Your Erroneous Zones* and *You'll See It When You Believe It*, while we waited for him to board a plane. The conversation turned to the subject of relationships, and Wayne leaned forward, pointed at me, and declared, "You need to write a book on relationships." I told him I had already entertained the idea. He advised that I go away by myself to my favorite spot, a place that would delight my soul, go with an outline, meditate, and write. He suggested Maui, knowing that I loved Hawaii. I knew that Maui, exceptionally beautiful, would be too much of a distraction for me. On Maui there are splendid art galleries, countless ocean activities, and gourmet restaurants. No, I should go to a quieter island. I would go to sleepy Molokai. I felt charged—I could feel energy moving through my body. I was filled with joy and enthusiasm.

Later that morning I spoke with my husband, and he gave me his hundred-percent support. I looked at my calendar for January, and amazingly, it was open enough that anything scheduled could easily be shifted to another date. I could really feel the energy surging now. I called the airlines and discovered that not only could I fly on the dates I wanted, but I could upgrade to first class with my frequent flier miles. I put a hold on a seat.

Next, where to stay on this non-touristy island. I had saved an issue of a magazine on Hawaii that my eye doctor had given me a month or two before. I turned to the back, where there were numerous listings for the major islands, but none for Molokai. I was about to discard the magazine in disappointment when I saw a small ad, "Accommodations All Islands," and an 800 number. I called and told the woman who answered what I wanted: My desire was to be as close to the ocean as possible. I needed a table on which to write, a large picture window, a full kitchen, and a comfortable bed. She informed me that she knew of the perfect place; she would check on the dates and get back to me. She also told me that the place she had in mind was a number of miles from the only town and I would need a car, for which she would find the best rate.

With these travel arrangements in progress, I started brainstorming what areas I wanted to cover in my book. What would make it different from other relationship books? What could I say that was new and thought-provoking? Time passed as I contemplated and wrote, and then the telephone interrupted. It was the woman calling to let me know that everything was arranged, including the inter-island flight. I called the airline and reserved the seat from the mainland to Honolulu and back. By the end of the day everything was taken care of and confirmed.

When I had driven Wayne Dyer to the airport early that

morning, I could have had no idea how the day would unfold. Now I was going to Molokai, and that was only the beginning. I would write there, and the end result would be my first book, *A Course in Love*.

The Universe loves to support us in a grand manner. All we have to do is step aside and allow the wonder to unfold. My trip to Molokai was magical, filled with inspiration, flowing with creativity. Every day was bliss. It took me years to learn, but I finally knew how to turn the details over to the Universe and accept its complete support. Its twelve Laws cooperated in that one event in my life:

FAITH: I had already begun to entertain the idea of writing a book. I knew I was capable.

DIVINE PURPOSE: I knew I was to be an author on relationships and living a magnificent life.

CONSCIOUSNESS: I felt charged and could feel the energy flowing through my body. Thoughts and feelings were connected.

VISION: When Wayne Dyer told me I needed to write a book on relationships, he was confirming an idea already in place in me.

JOY: The idea filled me with joy and enthusiasm. I was living in bliss.

POWER: I took charge, and all arrangements quickly fell into place.

LOVE: I felt Divine Love caressing me at every moment.

WISDOM: I was filled with creativity and inspiration that I knew needed expression.

NON-ATTACHMENT: I was simply surrendering to God's plan for me.

ABUNDANCE: A great increase in my financial good was going to occur.

FORGIVENESS: Writing *A Course in Love* would give me an opportunity to reexamine my most important forgivenesses.

DIVINE LIFE: I was always recognizing God as my life.

All the experiences surrounding *A Course in Love* were the culmination of years of preparation, forgiveness, healing, studying, learning, and teaching.

A simple truth of Spiritual Law is that what is possible for one is possible for all. You too can fully engage the laws and express your uniqueness. Then they become who you are rather than what you hope to be, and you actively live as a Spiritual Being, in a Spiritual Universe, governed by Spiritual Law.

Twelve Spiritual Laws Meditation

To live such an extraordinary life takes unyielding commitment, focus, and clear intention. You must engage all you have come to know as the truth of your being. This means you are successful, fulfilled, and confident, and live in love, peace, and joy. You may still live where you have always lived and work where you have always worked, but you will be different. You will be happy. You will live as a person who understands how richly blessed your life is and how close you are to the heartbeat of life. You will remember your sacred nature. The following meditation will help reinforce all that you know and are still learning.

Phase 1

This will take from thirty to forty-five minutes. Prepare the space by lighting a white candle, or burning a stick of incense, or placing a single-stemmed flower in front of you. Have the clear intention that you are creating a sacred space.

Remove your shoes. Wear loose, comfortable clothing. Take

the telephone off the hook or turn off the ringer. Arrange your seat or meditation cushion for maximum comfort. If you like music in the background, select a gentle, themeless recording with nature sounds or synthesized music. Make sure it is at least forty-five minutes long, so you don't interrupt your focus during the meditation.

Phase 2

This phase usually takes between ten and fifteen minutes.

When you and the space are prepared, take your seat. Turn on the music. Take three gentle, deep breaths and clear your mind. Release every thought, allowing your mind to become a vast pool. Relax your body, beginning with your scalp and slowly moving down your entire body. Visualize each external and internal body part and tell it silently: *Relax*. Breathe deeply. *Relax*. Feel all tension draining out of your body through your fingertips and the soles of your feet each time you exhale and relax more and more deeply. *Relax* into the meditation. Continue this phase until you feel totally at peace.

Phase 3

During this phase you will be engaging and communing with each of the twelve Spiritual Laws. This will be done in an aware yet detached way. The order here is that of the preceding chapters. You may change it if you like.

While breathing slowly, peacefully bring to mind the idea of FAITH. Take a deep breath in, and as you do so think, *I breathe in FAITH*. Hold that thought for a moment. Allow FAITH to bathe your soul in light. As you exhale, think, *I breathe out FAITH, and I smile*. Rest for a moment and then continue. On the in breath, *My FAITH is growing like a tree*. On the out breath, *My FAITH is irreversible, and I smile*. Rest for another moment and connect on a soul level with FAITH.

After several moments take a deep breath in. As you do so, think, *I breathe in my* DIVINE PURPOSE. Hold that thought for a moment. Allow your Divine destiny to be tapped. Then as you exhale, *I breathe out my* DIVINE PURPOSE *into the world, and I smile*. Rest for a moment as you feel the connection. On the in breath, *My* DIVINE PURPOSE *is written in the heavens*. On the out breath, *My* DIVINE PURPOSE *is written in my soul, and I smile*. Consciously connect yourself with the energy of your DIVINE PURPOSE. After several moments move on.

Take another deep breath in, and as you do so, think, *My thoughts and feelings are clear and true*. On the out breath, *My* CONSCIOUSNESS *is clear, vibrant, and creative, and I smile*. Rest in the clarity of your quickened CONSCIOUSNESS. On the in breath, *My* CONSCIOUSNESS *is like a clear pool*. On the out breath, *My* CONSCIOUSNESS *is vast and deep as the ocean, and I smile*. Be very still and tune in to the vastness of your CONSCIOUSNESS.

On the in breath, *I breathe in* VISION. On the out breath, *I breathe out* VISION, *and I smile*. Breathe deeply again, and on the in breath think, *My* VISION *is illuminated*. On the out breath, *I see all things truly, and I smile*. Pause and integrate your expanding awareness.

On the in breath, *I breathe in* JOY. On the out breath, *I breathe out* JOY, *and I smile*. Be still. Feel the JOY bubbling within you. On the in breath, *My* JOY *is like a bubbling brook*. On the out breath, *My* JOY *is contagious, and I smile*. Allow the sense of happy, joyous feelings to tingle through you. Pause and then move on.

On the in breath, *I breathe in unlimited* POWER. On the out breath, *I breathe out unlimited* POWER, *and I smile*. Rest and become totally comfortable in your POWER. On the in breath, *My POWER is stable and fluid.* On the out breath, *I know my POWER can move mountains, and I smile.* Feel your POWER expanding within your very cells. When you get a sense of this, move on.

On the in breath, *I breathe LOVE in.* On the out breath, *I breathe LOVE out, and I smile.* Bring your focus directly into your heart. On the in breath, *My LOVE is nurturing and accepting like a mother's for her child.* On the out breath, *My LOVE is universal and impersonal like the sun, and I smile.* Remain focused as you continue.

On the in breath, *I breathe in WISDOM.* On the out breath, *I breathe out WISDOM, and I smile.* On the in breath, *My WISDOM is honest and perceptive.* On the out breath, *My WISDOM guides me into truth, and I smile.* Sense yourself as a respected, wise, venerable soul.

On the in breath, *I breathe in NON-ATTACHMENT.* On the out breath, *I breathe out NON-ATTACHMENT, and I smile.* Let go of everything. Be concerned with nothing. On the in breath, *My mind is free and uncluttered.* On the out breath, *My mind is a vast circle clinging to nothing, and I smile.* Allow the sense of vastness to expand.

On the in breath, *I breathe ABUNDANCE in.* On the out breath, *I breathe ABUNDANCE out, and I smile.* Get a deep sense of how rich you are, in countless ways. On the in breath, *I am one with the Source of all ABUNDANCE.* On the out breath, *My Source is limitless like the stars in the sky, and I smile.* Bask in the ABUNDANCE of life. Feel how prosperous you are.

On the in breath, *I breathe FORGIVENESS in.* On the out breath, *I breathe FORGIVENESS out, and I smile.* Experience the deep sense of freedom that arises from nonjudgment and releasing all grievances. On the in breath, *My FORGIVENESS offers me peace and freedom*. On the out breath, *My* FORGIVENESS *blesses the world, and I smile*. Now send this idea of FORGIVENESS around the globe to enfold and bless everyone and everything on our planet.

On the in breath, *I breathe* DIVINE LIFE *in*. On the out breath, *I breathe* LIFE *out, and I smile*. Connect with the very life of God pulsating within our cells, through you, and around you. On the in breath, *My* LIFE *is whole and complete*. On the out breath, *My* LIFE *is ever-expanding energy, and I smile*.

Now simply breathe deeply and join in a blissful union with God, as you conclude the meditation. Take your time coming back. There is no need to hurry.

You are blessed.

You are loved.

You are holy.

You are limitless.

This course of life is a never-ending study. Here you have received a portion of what there is to learn. It is not the end, but it is a reminder of what is eternally true for you as a beloved child of God.

Rise now and take your rightful place as God's divine heir. May you come to know your true worth. God bless you.

Acknowledgments

My journey is deeply enriched by the dear ones with whom I share love and support. Your presence in my life is a joy beyond measure, and I offer thanks:

To all those who have supported me and believed in me—especially my parents, Jim and Vivian; my brother Jim and his wife, Vicki, my brother Perry; my longtime friends Susy Miller Schwabe, Ginna Bell Bragg, Nancy Miller, Pat McClain, Roger Goins, John Broad, Ronn Liller—thank you for your love through the years.

To my cousin Sharma Askov, for returning to my life, and being the daughter I never had.

To Felicia Hyde-Martinez, our church administrative assistant and my friend, for taking care of countless details and supporting me in communicating with a national audience.

To Julianne Filion, for being a magnificent assistant.

To my stepfamily, whom I adore—Robyn, Jeff, Christopher, and Samantha; Lisa, Joe, Benjamin, and Samuel; Julie and Tim. You are wonderful.

To my Master Mind partner and friend Marleen Davis.

A special thanks to my dear supporters at Unity Village, especially Reverend Chris Chenoweth, Reverend Michael Maday, and Reverend Phil White.

To Linda Spencer, my soul sister and teacher of unconditional love.

To my spiritual teachers Sister Augustine, O.P., Dr. Jean Houston, and His Holiness the Dalai Lama.

To my precious and wise friend Lama Chonam.

To my loving and conscious congregation, Unity of Greater Cleveland, for your support and willingness to let me reach beyond our doors to a larger community of seekers.

To Dan Wakefield, who truly knows what support means.

To my literary agent, Anne Sibbald, for being marvelous to me. I appreciate you so.

To Tina Bennett and Maria Gallacher at my agency, for taking such splendid care of important details.

To my former editor, Lisa Bach, for being such a treasure. I will always value our work and our dinners together.

A warm thanks to Tony Hudz and all at Audio Renaissance for their outstanding product and support.

To the staff at Tarcher/Putnam, especially Jocelyn Wright, Maria Liu, and Ken Siman, for enthusiastically welcoming me into your fold.

To Joel Fotinos, publisher at Tarcher. Our first meeting was by divine appointment, and our connection has only deepened through the years. We are of the same soul family. I appreciate and respect you totally.

To my literary assistant, Joan Kirkwood Miley. We work together as one mind. You are a treasure and dear friend.

To my husband, David S. Alexander—the love of my life, soulmate, gift from God, and still the very best manifestation of Spiritual Principles—for your love and willingness to do whatever was needed to assist in birthing this book. I am eternally grateful for your encouraging me to reach higher and stretch further than ever.

To Jen'ai, our kitty companion who brings such joy.

To the Holy Spirit, for years of inspiration and guidance, and for the love that enfolds me in all that I do.

Lectures and Workshops with Joan Gattuso

Joan Gattuso's writing is equaled, and perhaps even surpassed, by her inspirational lectures and workshops for audiences throughout the United States and Canada. Her style is loving, warm, humorous, and entertaining, yet powerful and motivational, and always inspirational.

People's lives change after they attend Joan's presentations and follow the principles she teaches about holy relationships and about creating the life they have dreamed of.

For information about booking Joan for a presentation, or for a schedule of her lectures and workshops, or a catalogue of available tapes, call 1-800-2LOVEU2 (256-8382), or write: Joan Gattuso Presentations, PO Box 22685, Beachwood, OH 44122.

About the Author

Joan Gattuso is a powerful spiritual teacher and author who has touched people nationwide with her unique loving style of presentation and writing. She assists individuals in finding the true meaning of love and their purpose in life. The author of the best-selling *A Course in Love,* she is the minister of Unity of Greater Cleveland. She resides in a Cleveland suburb with her husband, David Stuart Alexander, also an author.